T0146664

The Great Wing

THE
Great

Wing

A PARABLE

LOUIS A. TARTAGLIA, M.D.

BEYOND
WORDS
Publishing
I N C

Beyond Words Publishing, Inc.
20827 N.W. Cornell Road, Suite 500
Hillsboro, Oregon 97124-9808
503-531-8700 · 1-800-284-9673

Cover design: Heather Speight and Fran Lee
Interior design and composition: Fran Lee
Cover and interior art: Larry Tucci
Managing editor: Kathy Matthews
Proofreader: Marvin Moore

Printed in the United States of America
Distributed to the book trade by Publishers Group West

Library of Congress Cataloging-in-Publication Data
Tartaglia, Louis A.
   The great wing : a parable / Louis A. Tartaglia.
   p. cm.
   ISBN: 978-1-58270-332-0
   1. Geese—Fiction. I. Title.
PS3570.A6566G74   1999
813'.54—dc21   98-48467
                                         CIP

The corporate mission of Beyond Words Publishing, Inc.:
   Inspire to Integrity

To my wife, Barbara,
and the Great Wing essence within her.

A very special thanks to
Wayne and Marcie Dyer,
who encouraged me to risk writing
in spite of my fears,
and many thanks to the late
Og Mandino and his wife, Bette,
who listened and always suggested
I send it out again.
Thanks for believing.

Contents

Foreword

The late Mother Teresa of Calcutta suggested that
The Great Wing *be published in Italian by Rizzoli.*
This is a translation of the foreword to that edition.

At first glance, *The Great Wing* might seem like an expression of the New Age culture, but in reality it belongs to the new consciousness that is expanding in the world, including the currently popular concept of recovery.

The volume is a complement to the parable of *Jonathan Livingston Seagull*, and it reveals the various phases of transformation of an individual goose, Gomer, while he passes from the limitations of his own ego into a sense of community with the flock.

Through crises of self-esteem, of credibility, and of motives surrounding his own existence, the transcendence of his ego leads him to the "Flock Mind." In this new inner worldview, Gomer can reach "Density One," which, as the book describes, is nothing other than the simple joining of the individual into the collective consciousness. This allows

Gomer and the flock to take off on the grand migratory flight, a symbol of the ultimate realization.

"At some time in their lives," the book reads, "all creatures doubt that they have been given the inner strength to fulfill their destinies. . . . 'The Great Wing is always there,' said Grandpa. 'It is your nature, your essence. It never leaves you. . . . It is essential to believe in yourself, but it is also essential to fly with those who believe in you too."

The great challenge in life is to become that which in essence we already are. To awaken the giant that sleeps inside us: this is the great duty!

Frequently I heard Mother Teresa say, "So as a seed is destined to become a tree, so we are also destined to grow into the same consciousness of Christ."

The postmodern period, which actually developed from the youth revolution of the '60s, has provoked the exploration of new inner spaces and new points of view, hastening the crises of values and credibility of our social-cultural system and religious system, crises that we brought on ourselves before the '60s, and particularly from the period after World War II.

While on one hand, in a negative sense, a lot of moral and ethical barriers were broken, such as those regarding sexuality and the frontiers of the mind and the subconscious with psychoactive drugs, yet in a positive sense, the whole spiritual world in us was rediscovered, and it claimed us.

By *spirituality*, I don't necessarily mean formal religion. One can follow formal religion and still be void of spirituality, or one can be spiritual without ever joining a formal religion; I personally believe, like Étienne Gilson, the French philosopher, that good paths lead to the gospel.

In the last forty years or so, through the media, journeys to the East, and experiments of every kind, the young have put into action other forms of perceptions of the spirit, union with the divine, the Ultimate Reality. Beyond the concepts and the familiar terms of our Judeo-Christian faith, there are popular notions that the same spiritual reality exists in other forms, in other cultures, even older and sometimes deeper than our systems.

The Universal law that governs every existence, and which in the philosophy of the Vedanta was called *Sanatha Dharma*, describes none other than that which we call, in perhaps a more personal sense, Divine Providence, and in this book, the Great Wing.

Our duty, all things considered, aside from our different paths, is to realize in time and in the space of our individuality what Saint Ignatius of Loyala called, in his book *Spiritual Exercises*, "the purpose for which we were created."

If we don't satisfy this deep necessity of being, we will always be divided within ourselves, running behind our superficial desires and neglecting to remember our deeper needs.

This discrepancy with ourselves will never allow us to find the synergy that makes us enter into the "Density One" and that allows us to take the flight of the Great Wing to the transcendence of our ego, the transcendence of the world of senses, in the freedom of the absolute of God, and with that plenitude which will never wear out.

The Great Wing points out a path of belief and recovery that stimulates readers to question themselves on the great mysteries of existence. Through all the many stages of growth, the great voyage consists of reaching a goal of integration and realization of oneself.

Finally, some words about the author. Doctor Tartaglia is a dear friend from whom I have learned many things. He introduced me to various systems of recovery that he was working with, such as psychiatric medicine, to treat the various forms of dependence and mental illness and spiritual illness that inflict the individuals of our time.

We met, by one of the strange contrivances of the "great mandala" that is Divine Providence, in the "Mother House" of the Missionary Sisters of Charity in Calcutta.

It was specifically Mother Teresa who brought us together. A recovery center for drug addiction was being organized not far from the "Mother House," on Lenin Serani street, and I was looking for skilled help. Mother Teresa asked Doctor "T" to come to paint and clean the designated rooms in the center. Doctor "T" instead thought that he could do something better for me, and he invited me into his hotel for a beautiful lunch that I really needed. He spoke to me about the various systems of recovery and the spiritual beliefs that he knew about. He illustrated to me in a profound manner the system of the "Twelve Steps" that are applied to various types of dependence and that are most popularly known by the members of A.A. (Alcoholics Anonymous).

He explained to me another system of belief called the "Master Mind," which developed in Michigan from the Church of Today, a concept that made a particular impression on me and received the most results with the first group of people together in Calcutta.

From this meeting was born a friendship that lasts still and that on many occasions has been a reciprocal stimulus in the face of the great existential flight.

This is how I am certain that *The Great Wing* will be a stimulus and a spiritual awakening for many people who are seeking the inner path and searching for completion, imperceptibly, step by step, one day at a time, something that they, like Gomer, the protagonist of this work, had never before dared to hope for. This book, in truth, is just a simple parable that contains a powerful message: an invitation to total wholeness, which is the process of synergy that introduces the individual to the spirit of the flock and allows people to realize the journey of the Great Wing.

Father Angelo Scolozzi
Servant Leader
Missionaries of Charity, Third Order

1

The Struggle to Surrender

For thousands of years, flocks of geese have been flying in unison from the Northern Lakes to their winter homes in Chesapeake Bay. No flock has ever flown more than a few miles without naturally forming flight patterns. And when migration occurs, the flight patterns become very special.

Scientists have tried to explain the aerodynamics of geese flight patterns, but they still do not understand how these patterns are established. The whole flock instinctively creates a "V" formation, almost like one giant bird.

There is a lesser and a greater wing in the formation. The left side is of lesser strength and is shorter. The lesser wing is manned by the older, infirm birds and by those that are too young to work the greater wing. The stronger birds are able to sustain the phenomenal stress of flying in the greater wing. They bring the flock safely to their new home, a place prepared for them when autumn arrives.

For every animal in nature, the changing of the seasons has a different meaning. To the young, it represents the wonder of the many *faces of life. To the old, it brings a sense of reassurance in the constancy of change. For a young goose named Gomer, the change of seasons, though marked by wonder, caused a stirring in his heart that left him feeling uneasy.*

All summer, nature had seemed unwavering, but now the days were getting shorter and the evenings growing longer. Gomer Goose had noticed that the leaves were turning many shades of red and gold. There was unusual activity in the flock. Grandpa Goose had been trying to get Gomer to go to flock training, to take the lessons that all geese must learn before their first migration.

To Gomer, the idea of discipline was repulsive; there just didn't seem to be any merit in it. Flying meant being free—free from life's problems, free from responsibility, just plain free!

He refused to accept the idea of learning to get the Flock Thought into his mind. He wasn't really sure that he wanted to leave the area of the Northern Lakes anyway. The summer had been so much fun. He had hung around with the other geese and had had a wonderful time frolicking in the water, fishing, and playing all day. The days were getting shorter, though, and the weather seemed to be getting colder.

The older geese kept talking of flying to another bay, but because it was so far away, he tired just thinking about the long trip. And then there was this Flock Thought that he just didn't understand. Sometimes the older ones called it Flockmindedness, and others called it the Flock Mind. Since it had so many names, how was he to understand what Grandpa called "just one big idea"? How could he fly with them if he really didn't have a grasp of what they were talking about?

For the past few days, he had seen the other geese talking. They would get together and discuss their visions of the beautiful new home that Nature was preparing for them. Every cycle she did this, yet in Gomer's mind there was no guarantee that this event was going to happen again. The older members of the flock seemed to be certain that their winter home was waiting for them. They told Gomer that they intuitively knew and were convinced of its beauty and readiness.

Gomer was skeptical. It just couldn't be. Grandpa had warned him that he must fly south with them or suffer in the cold weather and experience immeasurable hardships. The geese who stayed behind were never seen or heard from again. The shelters that the stragglers built never seemed to last through the winter; they were destroyed when the great freeze came. Even though Gomer had his doubts about going, he could see from the activity of the flock that just about everyone believed that it was better to make the migration than to remain. A strange time it was, the changing of the seasons, and it made Gomer feel a certain pressure to do something, even though he wasn't certain what it was. No matter what he did, he never felt that he was prepared for the long flight.

For some time, Grandpa had been grooming Gomer for the migration. Gomer had heard numerous stories of how the geese would develop the Flock Thought to such intensity that the migration would become automatic, but he didn't believe them. Grandpa understood Gomer's dilemma. In a comforting voice he had said, "Not to worry, little one. When the time comes for the great migration to our winter home, your natural instincts will enable you to develop the Flock Thought." Gomer could hear his grandfather's words echoing in his mind.

2

Density One

Bombarded by all these facts and ideas, Gomer was skeptical about the notion that Density One would be reached. He was even more skeptical that the flock would then spontaneously form specific migratory flight patterns. Gomer had two major problems with this idea. First, no one was able to explain to him how this incredible process called Density One occurred. Second, he wasn't even sure what they meant when they discussed the concept of migration. All he knew, from the discussions of distance and air speeds at the older birds' group meetings, was that it must be a lot of hard work. He suspected that it was very dangerous and that the whole flock was leaving itself vulnerable to a vast assortment of unforeseen problems.

As he paddled quietly around the pond, he thought about the Density One phenomenon. He repeatedly asked himself, "What is it really, and how is it done? Will I even understand it when it happens? Couldn't I just continue practicing the types of flying that I already know?" His grandfather had told him it was quite all right to learn other forms of flying—to slow himself down and speed up, to play on the pond, to frolic and to exercise his wings.

"That is all well and good," he could hear Grandpa say. "But there comes a time when what you learn must be used to ensure the survival of the whole flock into another season!"

"Grandpa sure was serious," he thought. "In order to ensure the survival of the flock into the new season, I must share what I have learned with the other birds. But there is nothing wrong with this season. Why should I bother to change anything? I just want to stay and play!" With that, a cold wisp of wind lightly reminded him that the seasons were changing. He approached the shore and continued to muse about all the new information being presented to him.

"In any case," he said to himself, "this Density One that Grandpa spoke about will supposedly be reached when enough birds entertain the thought of migration and the Flock Mind is held simultaneously by a large enough proportion of the flock." Of course, these were only fancy words to Gomer. "I guess it simply means that when a lot of us geese start worrying enough about leaving, something is bound to happen." But he was sure of only one thing: that he didn't understand it all. He was almost certain that he preferred to stay behind, and this thought made him feel lonely.

The Great Ones of the flock always made the trip and always seemed to return. They enjoyed the good times they had each summer, but they still had to endure this terribly long flight. They seemed to like it, though—it was more than just OK. From what they said, it seemed that once you were really into it, once you really got going, you could fly for days as effortlessly as a wisp of smoke from a chimney. Obviously, there was a secret to the effortless flight of the Great Ones. Gomer wondered what that secret was and if he would be able to learn it.

3

The Great Wing

*L*ike most geese, Gomer had been raised in the Northern Lakes region, an enchanted land of forests, ponds, and streams, nestled in the lovely foothills of the Laurentian Mountains. In winter, the lakes lie dormant beneath a soft, silent blanket of snow as they wait for Mother Nature's power to imbue them with life. In spring, the season when Gomer was born, the land sparkles from clear mountain dew on the grass of small meadows surrounding the lakes. Flowers suddenly abound, blossoming to herald the birth of the young geese. The little birds learn to play in these cool waters amid a changing cascade of spring colors. Life is easy for the young of the flock. Nature entertains them with her endless distractions and provides what their minds and bodies need in order to grow.

By their very essence, the Northern Lakes nurture life. They flow with an abundance of all that is necessary for survival. It is in this special environment that young geese innocently spread their wings in their first attempt at flying. As spring transforms itself into the heat of summer, the bodies of the young geese metamorphose into powerful *instruments capable of graceful flight on the northern winds, and as the seasons changed, the naive Gomer was transformed into a strong young bird. With only a hint of provocation, his instinct to fly would drive him up into the cool northern air.*

Nature has blessed geese with the ability to maneuver the wind, a potential that young geese seldom realize. The older ones know that it takes at least one migration to learn to tap into their potential. Migration teaches the young that unity is essential. If left alone, the young geese would not be able to learn this skillful movement so quickly. But they are surrounded by their families and friends, who possess a fierce loyalty. In other words, geese bond together; they flock. At sunset, formations of geese can be seen moving along the horizon, seeming to float amid the purple and gold as day passes into night.

This phenomenon of the flock is an expression of the power of nature—or the Great Wing, as geese call it. When a flock takes to the air in a migration, the fittest of the geese fly in the greater wing. Gomer knew that he was supposed to fly in the greater wing. The major difference between the greater and the lesser wing is that the birds of the greater wing rotate. The last bird slowly moves up the line until he becomes the lead bird. Then he is flying at the peak, or point position. The greater wing is the power wing, and the lesser wing drafts the greater. In this formation, the rear bird is always drafting the bird in front of it. This is all under the control of the Great Wing nature of geese. All geese are capable of this formation.

At some time in their lives, all creatures doubt that they have been given the inner strength to fulfill their destinies. But no one has been cheated; no one is shortchanged, though some believe they are.

Gomer, too, asked himself the eternal question, "Do I have what it takes?" and a part of him feared the answer. He had almost resigned himself to the fact that he would stay behind. He believed he was not emotionally ready for the migration of the flock. He wanted to live out his days in fun and peace and not have to go through the training with the other birds.

"I'm just going to stay," he thought. Suddenly he felt a blast of cold air and caught his grandfather giving him a wise look. Somehow, Gomer felt he could trust Grandpa, who seemed to be so understanding and loving. Gomer believed everything that his grandfather told him and noticed that others in the flock often came to ask his view on what was happening.

"The Great Wing is always there," said Grandpa. "It is your nature, your essence. It never leaves you. We sometimes think that this is not so when one of our leaders passes on or someone joins another flock. Sometimes we fear it is gone because our numbers diminish or grow too fast for our own thinking. But as soon as formation starts and the great flight begins, we all realize that the Great Wing has been within us all the time. It forms itself through us and with us, and no matter which part of the wing you fly in, you will always be in the right place in flight at the right time."

Gomer thought this was nonsense. He looked at his own wing and wondered, "If my feathers all had a mind of their own, would they be able to form a wing and fly in formation?" Yet instinctively he knew that they couldn't, that his present understanding was not enough. His wing would turn into an aerodynamic disaster!

His grandfather was explaining the Flock Mind and the Great Wing. "If you try to do this type of flight alone, you will fail. Your frustration will over-whelm you. Sometimes that is precisely what you need to have happen. You need to stop trying to understand by the way you think. As a single goose, you have the ability to do alone what the Great Wing does together, only in a limited way. But that's OK, because it needs to be that way. The power of the Great Wing, with its range and ability to travel at high speeds without effort, can only be learned with the flock in migration. It is a special time, a time to realize the Great Wing within."

Grandpa continued speaking in a matter-of-fact tone. "You must also believe that the Great Wing will form. I don't know why, but the change in seasons seems to focus everyone's attention on the Flock Mind and helps them to believe. The idea that the Great Wing will form is so intensified that you can't help feeling the change in the air. The wind seems to flow in the precise direction needed to assist the initial flight pattern. Logically, you'll know that the wind hasn't changed, though your perception of it will have.

"As the level of belief intensifies, more of the birds start to allow their flight to shift spontaneously from simple self-control to a free form of high-intensity, Flock Mind flying called hyperflight. You start to realize that your whole being has within it all the equipment needed to shift into high gear and really take off!"

Grandpa paused for a moment and looked off toward the horizon. "It's such a rush! You are filled with an energy, a vitality, a feeling so powerful that it draws out resources you never knew you had. You suddenly realize that you can endure flying at hyperflight speeds effortlessly." He smiled at Gomer. "All you need is for only one other goose to believe in you when you're flying and the Great Wing will release your hyperflight potential.

"It is essential to believe in yourself," Grandpa said quickly, "but it is also essential to fly with those who believe in you too. You have to hook up with geese who believe that you can attain the Flock Mind and join them. Please know, Gomer, that we believe in you even when you seem to be faltering." Grandfather Goose became very sincere. "Don't be fooled by appearances. The Great Wing may cause what looks like faltering flight, but it really is a repositioning to your advantage. You will need to remember this at various times during your training and the migration.

"A few seasons back, a lovely young goose joined our flock. Her attractiveness in solo flight turned quite a few heads. But when the migration started, this gorgeous creature went from poetry in motion to what looked like the dance of disaster. Time after time, she fought bravely to control what looked like a malfunctioning body. We all learned through her that it is the adversity, the struggle, that nurtures the seed of one's true potential. We realized that despair can be the gateway to fulfillment. We learned that to develop our inner strength, we have to risk appearing weak to others. As we watched her struggle with her development, we came to see that only through the passage of humility could come true greatness. The metamorphosis was not easy for her, but her trials and tribulations allowed, or rather, guaranteed, her ultimately to become Gracious Goose."

"Sometimes you look as though you're going through the most uncomfortable alterations in flying habits and you appear so awkward," said Gracious Goose as she approached the wise old bird and his pupil. "I happen to be at a stage now where everything I do looks easy, but as Grandfather says, it wasn't always this way. There were times when I would falter and fall out of formation. My feathers would get quite ruffled, hindering me. I would seem to get all the way to the peak of the greater wing and not know which way I should shift to get back in formation and rest my tired wings. Then I would have to use so much energy to catch up with the flock that I could barely keep up.

"The funny thing is, though, that if you just trust your intuition, you'll ride a little draft of wind that will come at the precise time you leave the peak.

Then, if you relax, you'll only have to make minimal adjustments all the way to the back of the formation. The change from the front to the rear of the flock can be really quite exhilarating as you catch the draft of the last bird." She smiled as she recognized Gomer's fear. "You'll learn about the drop bird and adjustments in flight later. Just keep in mind that it's easy once the greater wing has picked you up after you have dropped from the peak."

"Gomer," said Grandpa, "just remember that at first when you feel really awkward, you are simply experiencing some temporary adjustments. While you are adapting, the Great Wing is subtly transforming you and enhancing your ability to enter into Flock Mind flight."

Grand Goose, the flock's most assertive character, strutted over. "Here's where the fun begins and when flight gets really interesting," he said. "Most of us thought that the only real exhilaration would be felt by the goose at the head of the flock. We all believed, at one time or another, that being at the peak was the easiest and most exciting time of the great flight."

"And that just wasn't so, as Grand Goose would know," interjected Grandpa. "Grand Goose is the strongest of the whole flock, and he didn't get that way by flying the tail!"

"The more you fly the peak, the harder you have to work," Grand Goose said bluntly. "There is no way out. If you're on the leading point of the greater wing, you face everything first. You must exert a great deal of energy in order to pave the way for the next goose to follow. If you don't, your energy could burn out quickly and your body could disintegrate at those speeds." He paused and then went on. "If you don't have the Flock Mind concentrated within you as you work your way up the greater wing, you won't be able to fly at peak. The Flock Mind is the force that protects your body and enables you to fly hyperflight speeds at the point." Grand Goose turned to Grandfather Goose. "Has he had instruction on moving up the greater wing?"

"Not yet," said Grandpa.

Grand Goose stopped for a moment. "Gomer, when you let go of the Flock Mind, even for an instant, all that you try to accomplish seems to get disturbed, and the winds of adversity thrash against you. Those same winds of adversity are the greatest teachers of strength, if only you can see them as such. The winds never change, but your perceptions will. You can be strengthened if you fly at the peak and stay in harmony with the Great Wing. I know, because that's the way it really is." He then turned and walked away, leaving behind a slightly confused Gomer with Grandfather and Gracious Goose.

4

Grand Goose, the Bravest of the Brave

"Grand Goose sometimes seems a little arrogant," said Grandpa, "but if you knew his story, you would understand why he struts around giving lessons to anyone who will listen. The title of Grand Goose is earned for one season and usually only once in a lifetime. It is a terrible trial that turns into a personal triumph. It is the greatest honor that can be accorded a goose after a great migration. Last season, it was that goose's honor and privilege to receive it.

"His name was Michael before the last migration. He didn't start out as the Grand Goose. He was just being himself. You see, Gomer," said Grandpa, "you don't set out on the great flight to become the Grand Goose. You're scared and nervous and just want to be able to maintain formation.

"I remember when I was a boy, which was a

wonderful time in my life. Flying solo was such a joy. Back then, I wasn't a grandfather. My youthful vigor surged through my wings and propelled me over the Northern Lakes at breathtaking speeds. I would roll and turn, or sometimes come diving in at the flock, then sharply bank and honk in sheer delight, knowing that the others were sure that I would crash. I thought that flying was only for fun and that the purpose of my wings was to see what kind of maneuvers I could accomplish in the sky. I liked the reprimands and the stern scoldings I received from my elders. I believed that they were in awe of me. Undoubtedly, my power was clear to them. I never realized, not even for a moment, that the power, the potential, and the instinct to control it was given to me for the overall good of the flock. I never thought I would have to use my strength to help others during a migration." His voice softened. "You know, Gomer, we never realize why we are here when we're learning the fundamentals of flight, but then the seasons change.

"When the time came, I did all the necessary work to learn the fundamentals and get ready for the migration. I was a little uneasy, but I was determined. Nothing was going to stop me, or so I hoped. My first migration was really scary stuff. I came through all right, but I shuddered every time I thought about who would become the Grand Goose. You see, Gomer, every year we hit one or two storms and the whole flock gets roughed up a bit. But there is always one storm that would kill us all if it weren't for the power of the Great Wing manifesting itself through the Grand Goose."

The old goose continued. "When a truly terrible storm hits, we can't rotate flight as we usually do. The lead bird gets stuck in the peak position. If he falters during the storm, he will lose his concentration, the whole flock's flight pattern will be broken, and all the birds will perish. No matter how desperate he may feel, he must remain the leader. The bird that survives in the point position during the most devastating tempest of the migration earns the title of Grand Goose.

"Gomer, before each migration every goose is told the same thing: 'You may not want to be the Grand Goose, but if a storm hits and you are in the lead position, you must stay until the storm ends. You will maintain the Flock Mind, because your life and that of the flock depend on your ability to hold the Flock Mind. You will allow the Great Wing to express itself in purity and maintain undying energy.'"

Grandfather Goose continued earnestly while looking into Gomer's eyes. "You will succeed in pulling the flock through." He paused. "You will rise to your greatness, and your ability to overcome will be an example for the whole flock to follow. You will perform great deeds but will humbly acknowledge that anyone can use this force." Grandfather Goose then stepped aside and started talking as though to an imaginary figure. "When I first received that message, I thought surely some other goose would be the Grand Goose. It couldn't possibly be me. I would never be able to hold the Flock Mind with such concentration and energy that I could fly as the lead bird through a storm!"

Gomer marveled and noticed how deeply alive Grandpa looked. The older goose was now facing Gomer again and was nodding his head as he spoke. Suddenly the thought came to Gomer that Grandpa was talking directly to his inner self. He kept silent while Grandpa went on.

"If a goose drops out of formation when a storm hits, he falters, drops, and cannot catch the draft of the last bird. The peak bird can't have the tail end of the greater wing shift down to pick him up if he is still trying to get the Great Wing thought into his mind. Thus the faltering bird falls out of formation and loses the flock. It doesn't end there, however," said Grandpa, seeing Gomer's look of concern. "The next bird in line can take the lead only through supreme effort and intense concentration. If he doesn't get too fatigued and his mind allows the purity of the Great Wing thought to manifest itself, he will struggle and gain the peak position."

Grandpa looked up to the sky and spoke slowly. "Then you have the challenge of leading the flock through the storm. If you accept the challenge, your whole life is transformed. If you don't and if you follow the bird that faltered, you are ringing your own death knell."

Grandfather Goose looked at Gomer. "After a

lead bird drops, it is only an exceptional bird that can retake the pole position in a storm. It is theoretically possible to maneuver the whole flock to pick up the bird that fell out of formation. Since this is so dangerous, only a truly great one will risk his life to catch a falling friend on his way down.

"To catch a friend who has fallen," said Grandpa, looking up again, "you must be certain that your mind can hold the truth of the Great Wing. You must also be certain that you have only love for your friend and no fear for yourself. It can be done." Grandpa was nodding his head slowly and solemnly.

"Last year, the Grand Goose led us through a terrible storm, and he did it easily. Usually, after every migration, the Grand Council representing all the flocks convenes. At this particular council, I remember telling him, 'You made it look so effortless. You maintained your poise and did what no one else did on that journey.' Grand Goose said that he did what anyone else would have done. One of the other birds pointed out to him that he chose his position in the flock and accepted every challenge that came with maintaining that position in formation. He thus chose to be the Grand Goose, and because of that, we saluted him.

"It was a wonderful Grand Council. Michael, the Grand Goose, was asked to speak, as all birds are once they have led the flock through a storm. You see, Gomer, in every migration, the Grand Goose has the responsibility of imparting more knowledge or wisdom to the flock. The Great Wing in essence speaks through the Grand Goose, not only in his flight but also verbally through him at the Grand Council. I remember when I was your age, little one. The Grand Goose for that migration taught us things about hyperflight that we had experienced only in that particular migration. Once the knowledge had been imparted, however, the flock retained it for its use in subsequent flights. Gomer, every so often there comes a time when a storm hits during the last hundred miles or so of the great migration. During these last miles all the flocks join together to produce one giant flock. If a storm hits at this time, the goose who leads us through the storm has the crucial task of imparting special knowledge to all the flocks at the Grand Council. Again, this is so rare you don't have to worry your head about it." Suddenly an icy blast of Canadian air ruffled his feathers.

Grand Goose had walked over and was listening to the story. He spoke softly. "I really didn't want to be the Grand Goose, but I didn't refuse it when I knew I must. I was afraid to fly when I first got started for exactly the same reasons that most geese are afraid to fly. I feared I was inadequate for the task. I wondered if I would be able to overcome the challenges that I would face. I avoided all thoughts of real leadership. My only concern was getting through the migration in one piece. Yet I found myself gradually going back to the Grand Goose stories I had heard in the past. I began to wonder if it was my turn this time. I was thinking about being the Grand Goose when I chose my spot in the formation." Grand Goose smiled gently and told Gomer how he had gone down to pick up his mate, Gracious Goose, after the flight had formed. "When you extend yourself to help someone you love and care for, it leads to many new and exciting experiences. This is especially true if it affects your position in the greater wing."

Gomer shuddered at another blast of ice-cold wind. Grand Goose continued. "During the whole flight, and even before we took off, my mind was filled with fantasies of the Grand Goose and visions of triumph over the storm. All through the flight I concentrated in a way that astounded me. I lost myself in a visual fantasy. I performed courageous maneuvers while I was in the head position, as the storm was with me. Eventually I had some doubts and worries and began to falter. I then realized that I had just dropped from the head of the flock. I pulled myself together and went on and again lost all track of place and time. It was beautiful, now that I remember it, but it was so scary then."

Grandpa then stepped in. "No Grand Goose ever felt comfortable with the thought of being a Grand Goose once he realized what it was and what the task meant. Isn't that right?" he asked Michael. "That's right," Gomer could hear himself thinking as Grand Goose nodded in agreement.

The crisp autumn chill of the northern winds brushed against Gomer's feathers. Suddenly he felt the need to fly, even for just a few minutes. Grand Goose looked at him and flapped his wings and honked. Gomer followed suit, and in a few short seconds they were airborne together.

"When I first learned about the Grand Goose," said Michael, "I realized how little I knew. I believed that I was totally inadequate for an important position in flight. I could trust my instinct to fly only occasionally. And I, like you, had instructors with me whenever I truly needed them."

They circled the lake in a slow climb. Gomer could see other little groups of geese practicing the new techniques they were learning together. In the distance, he could see four or five birds flying together in a small flock. They were practicing the acceleration to hyperflight. Everywhere he looked, there seemed to be activity. Gomer was drafting Grand Goose. They were flying fairly quickly, but they continued to stay in the climb. It was as though Grand Goose wanted him to get a better view of the entire flock.

Grand Goose then slowed his flight. "You can go back down now," he said to Gomer. "You're high enough to see the whole flock from here, and we can continue with the lesson."

Gomer picked a small area of the lake and splashed down. In his mind, he saw Grand Goose leading the flock through a terrible storm, the likes of which he had never known. Grand Goose looked at him and said gently, "I had the vision in me to be the Grand

Goose. At first, I thought I was dreaming about another bird, one far more courageous and disciplined than myself. In fact, I was seeing the me that I would become. It was so different from the me that I knew that I didn't recognize myself. Only later did I understand what my teacher meant when he pointed at me and said, 'You will be what your mind can see.'" Grand Goose was pointing at Gomer when he finished.

The intent look on Grand Goose's face suddenly became very loving. Gomer had realized that the idea of becoming a Grand Goose, though foreign to him at first, now seemed at least a possibility. He believed that some other exceptional bird would become the Grand Goose. He could see one of the older and stronger birds at peak pulling the flock through the storm. Just then, another cold blast of wind hit, and he shivered.

5

Gracious Goose and Bill

Gracious Goose swam over to give her lesson to young Gomer. "The Great Wing has been described by some of our scientists as a form of synergy. I'm not sure if any of the ordinary flock members understand these words. What it means is that two or more birds flying together in perfect harmony form a third mind, the Flock Mind." Gracious Goose realized that she needed to explain this further to Gomer so that he could understand what allows this to happen.

"Love acts as a bridge of energy between the minds of two individual geese. As soon as unconditional love is present and you accept all the others in formation with you as necessary parts of the whole, the Great Wing will become effortless for you. If you hold even one angry thought toward another goose or toward yourself, you will lose the Flock Mind and falter. The thoughts you hold deeply within are experienced as the winds of life as you fly. Hold thoughts of the Great Wing and love each and every bird for his part, and you will find that the wind will lift you with an ease that will astound you. You will be flying on the wings of love."

Gracious Goose paused and looked at Gomer and then slowly went on. "In reality, the winds of adversity are the thoughts of fear and resentment blowing back at you. As long as you think in fear, the adversity will continue."

Gomer sensed that they were trying to make him understand the teaching, but he just wasn't ready yet. With that, a blast of cold air lifted his feathers, and he felt a chill all the way down to his bones. He realized that it would be difficult for him if he didn't learn the training. After all, none of the geese that stayed behind were ever heard from again. He would have to give it some thought. For now, he was content to play in the lake and frolic with a few friends. He politely excused himself, and Gracious Goose and Grandpa nodded knowingly.

He went looking for his friends, but most of them seemed to be gone. They were off in special trainings or practicing the Great Wing formation. He was growing a little scared.

"When the great cold comes . . ." He heard Grandpa's words echoing in his mind. It seemed to have been so long since he first heard those words. "When the great cold comes, there will be a transformation both inside and out." He heard Grandpa's voice again. "Your feathers will thicken and your body will prepare itself for the long winter in Chesapeake. You will be able to feel the difference in your body. You will know that you are somewhat older and have now come of age."

He remembered the scene quite well. He and a few of his friends were talking to Grandpa. One little friend asked, "How will I know when I can get into the Flock Mind?" "How will I know when my mind is ready to experience the Great Wing?" asked another.

Gomer could see Grandpa now just as clearly as he did at the time when he spoke these strange words. "You will know when your outer circumstances seem to be changing around you and your old friends are not there to play with anymore. When you seem to come in contact only with geese who encourage you to take the Flock Mind training, you will be ready. It is as simple as that." Grandpa spoke quietly. "When the inner transformation has taken place, the outer world seems to be right in harmony, bringing you everything you need."

Just then Gomer's thoughts were interrupted. His friend Bill was playing nearby in the water. Gomer went over to talk. He loved Bill very much and wanted to ask his opinion of what to do. "Bill," he asked, "are you going to take the Flock Mind lessons and all that stuff?"

Bill looked at him quizzically. "What do you mean? I just assumed we all would, so I went ahead.

You know, Gomer," he said quickly, "you can do it if you want to. I've been working with Goosenstein, and what I've been able to learn in such a short time is incredible. He thinks I have everything it takes to be a Grand Goose. He has this whole thing down to a series of logical steps that need to be taken. I can sit around and listen to his explanations for hours."

Gomer became a little skeptical. He couldn't grasp Professor Goosenstein's teachings, and here was this young bird who seemed to have an understanding that was way beyond his own. He would have to see it to believe it.

Bill flapped his wings slightly as if to preen before Gomer. "I will be brought to the greater wing under the direct tutelage of Goosenstein."

"Oh, that's nice," said Gomer. "I guess it's important to have someone you relate to bringing you in when the migration starts."

"You're right," said Bill. "I guess you'll have Grandpa bring you in. It would only be fitting. He's the one you seem to understand the best."

"Yeah, but I don't understand how they do it," said Gomer.

Bill turned to his friend. "You need to attend some of the flock training sessions in order to learn. But as far as I can tell, the important thing is to hook up with the goose who is going to pull you in, and then you fly right in his draft. It gets exciting because you start to think, 'Flock yes!' Your flight accelerates and you catch the tail bird."

"Sounds pretty easy," interjected Gomer, but with a flat note in his voice.

"Well, that's not all of it," his friend said excitedly. "At the last moment, the bird you're drafting has to leave the lead position and drop back. You then wind up in position in the greater wing, just in front of the bird that brought you. The puller bird falters on purpose so that you can catch the draft of the last bird. And do you know why?" he asked enthusiastically. Gomer shook his head. "The puller bird is thinking of the Great Wing, and in order to be in harmony with the other birds, he has to let go of the thought and be part of the body of the greater wing and not be the peak bird. He was thinking 'Great Wing' so that they could get into hyperflight and he would be in autoflight. Now the puller bird and the bird he's bringing in are both going at a tremendous speed."

"Wait! Stop!" said Gomer with a little anger in his voice. "You're going too fast and I'm confused."

"OK, OK," he continued slowly and explained. "One bird at the head of the greater wing begins to chant, 'Great Wing, Great Wing,' which facilitates the process. The rest of the geese assist and support that bird by thinking about being the entire flock. This enables the lead bird to direct the whole flock's flight pattern. So now, if a bird at the end starts to think the peak-position chant, he will be out of harmony. As you know, Gomer, the peak bird is in autoflight, which is like having your flying controlled by an infinite intelligence. He is thinking the chant 'Great Wing' and his wings are beating powerfully in harmony with his internal rhythms. His body is filled with enormous energy and begins to glow. He directs the flight of the bird behind him by visualization. At this point, the puller bird must falter and allow the bird he's pulling to move right into the draft of the last bird in the greater wing. After he falters, he then gets picked up at the tail position right behind the bird he brought in."

Gomer grew silent. Didn't anyone understand that he just wanted to play and not have to think about these things? While he was daydreaming and sulking, Bill flew over to the other side of the lake and joined another discussion group.

6

August and Doubts

August approached Gomer slowly. "Things sure are changing around here," he said. Gomer looked up and saw his old friend. August appeared sad. "I am going to stay around for the winter," he said. "It can't be all that bad. There will probably be enough food for me when everybody else leaves. I can find shelter over by the old hunters cove," he muttered.

Gomer grew sadly quiet. He knew that August was planning to stay. He had heard the others talk about it, and he feared for his friend. His fear was interrupted by August's voice. "I really believe that all this stuff about the long flight, the Great Wing, and the Flock Mind is unnecessary. I've been able to find food all along and I'm always warm enough, so I'm staying behind."

"But those who stay never make it through the winter!" Gomer heard himself say in a pleading tone.

"Gomer, I don't believe I can get the Flock Mind or fly in formation," his old friend confessed sadly. "I've tried it numerous times and I've failed."

"But August," said Gomer, "they say we shouldn't do it alone, that of course we'll fail unless we work with someone who believes in us totally."

"I know, but I'm too embarrassed and I'm afraid that I'll fail if I try it. I really just need to get myself together a little more. Then maybe I'll be willing to ask for help." August was dejected.

"You have to be willing to ask for help." Gomer could hear the words plainly now as he saw Grand Goose speaking to one of the smaller training groups. "I wonder why that is so important," he mused, recalling the other times he had heard it said. His thoughts returned to August. If August were unable to ask for help, he would not make the long flight. Life, as he knew, was going to change drastically, and August would surely face a series of life-threatening adversities. There was the great cold. There would be the plant and lake freeze. There would come the great hunger and finally the snow burial, whatever that was. It all sounded pretty bad.

Just then he noticed some gray fluffy clouds on the horizon and a few flakes of snow. These were called flurries, and his crazy Uncle Ernest had tried to explain how they portend a definite change in the weather. "It lasts only a few minutes now, but later when we are no longer here, the snow will fall for days," he had said.

August started talking, and Gomer shifted his attention back to him. "I don't believe we can do it, Gomer Goose." There was a feeling of discouragement in the air as he confessed his fear to Gomer. "I don't really believe it, and I'm so scared. Each time I start to say this, our friends seem to avoid me." August went on to describe how the younger geese who had taken the training would almost run away when he started to voice his fears. No one, it seemed, wanted to listen to his doubts except a few older birds. Then August started to complain. "And the older birds aren't really listening. They just pick apart my excuses and refuse to understand my special circumstances."

Gomer felt a shudder go through him. He started to wonder if he had special circumstances that would keep him from maintaining the Flock Mind or from flying in the greater wing. He suddenly felt alone and afraid. He realized that he might not do the training, and if he didn't, his reasons for not taking the long flight would surely be misunderstood.

"No one really knows exactly what I'm going through," August went on. "I would take the flight training, but I don't believe they understand how difficult it is for me."

Gomer started to agree and felt his energy slowly diminishing. He was frightened just listening to

August and wanted to leave him. He started to hop up and down and waddled onto the shore to play. He encouraged his friend to follow. He knew that if he acted carefree, his friend would stop talking to him and leave him alone. He knew that he needed to get away from August.

"They will support you and encourage you, and at this time in your life, you will realize that you can no longer listen to geese who don't believe in your abilities without feeling a terrible pain inside." Grand Goose's words echoed in his mind. He wondered if it was happening to him. Could it be that the internal shift was taking place and that he was starting to see it outside of himself?

He had to stop and think about this Flock Mind training. Just then he felt another cold wind and noticed how strange the autumn sky looked in the evening. Every time he stopped to think, he felt a subtle push from Nature.

All around him there were reminders that the summer was over and that it was time to prepare for the great flight.

7

Powerlessness and the Release from Fear

Grandpa waddled over to Gomer. "He may shake from side to side and his body is old, but there is a real dignity to the way he carries himself," Gomer thought. He looked lovingly at Grandpa. He wanted to cry. He wanted to tell Grandpa that he was frustrated. No matter what he did to try to stop it, he could see that the world was changing around him. He was experiencing a feeling of powerlessness. Life was disorganized and unmanageable, or so it seemed. There was so much to do and so little time. He wanted to tell Grandpa that he had been trying to get into hyperflight and autoflight. He knew that he needed help. He knew that he just couldn't do it alone. He needed the help of the Great Wing and the other members of the flock.

Suddenly Grandpa started talking. Gomer could

feel the concern in his voice. "You may not understand this, Gomer, but when I was your age I too
wanted to do it alone. I didn't want to admit that the
Great Wing instinct was within me. I didn't want to
have to depend on the flock. I wanted to do it my
way. The great cold started to come, and I was feeling
desperate." Grandpa looked closely at Gomer and
continued. "Try to understand, Gomer. I've been
there," he said. "I know you need help. I can see it
and I know you don't want to admit it, but you've
already admitted it to yourself.

"There is a power within you that will give you
whatever you need to accomplish the great flight. The
Great Wing loves you and cares for you. It will help
you to fly. It will move your body in any way that is
necessary in order to complete the great migration. It
will allow you to do whatever is needed for you to fly
at peak, in full force, and with an awesome power that
is unknown to you at present. It will give you a
strength beyond that of an ordinary goose in flight. It
will give you more than you expect. It will help you to
do the necessary things that you weren't even aware
you could do. The Great Wing is love, and it loves
you. But it can only bring the whole flock to our winter home by working through you. The Great Wing
working through you is a miracle of Nature's love.
Don't you believe that?"

Gomer felt his body shivering. He started to cry.
He knew that he believed, but he disliked the idea of
admitting it. Another icy gust of wind hit him. He

also didn't like the way the weather made him feel as though he were losing control. "If I could just believe that my situation weren't so special and that everyone really understood me, I'd ask for help," he thought.

Grandpa continued on as if he could read Gomer's thoughts. "Your situation in many ways reminds me of my early days. I thought no one had experienced this change before, even though the trainers were all telling me that they had been there. I believed that I was a special case, and at the same time I knew that I wasn't. I thought I was going crazy. I waited until it got very cold, when I thought it was too late to ask for help and go through the training. I figured that I had blown it. I was angry with myself, and I had lost all hope of making the great flight. I was ready to face death."

Grandpa's story seemed so much like his own life that Gomer wanted him to continue. "You'd like me to go on?" It was a statement and a question at the same time. Gomer was feeling confused about everything, but he needed to hear what Grandpa had to say.

"I took the training and made the flight. The power of the Flock Mind was so intense that I learned quickly . . . but perhaps even too quickly," he added as an afterthought. "Though I seemed to handle the flight to the new bay with ease, I almost had major air disasters. It was quite a tumultuous time in my life," said Grandpa. "I didn't know that the longer you wait, the greater the recovery. I didn't know that I would be plagued by self-doubt for a few seasons. The earlier you start, the smoother the transition."

He paused and thought. "Some geese are not really aware of the transition into Flock Mind. They don't consciously believe in it. They just do it. They may even deny it, but they form the greater wing regardless."

Grandpa raised himself up to emphasize his next point. "The longer it takes for you to let go and let the Great Wing flow through you, the greater your recovery will be." He took a long breath and continued. "Sometimes, when a goose evolves at this stage, he may experience a tremendous struggle, since his life will be used as a heroic example for others to follow." Now Grandpa was looking at him directly. "This is why you're in turmoil. The truly great ones always are." He paused. "It is not that you can't do it— it is because you will attain the Flock Mind so intensely that your struggle will be an inspiration for others."

Gomer's body started to shake. He could feel the sobs being released from his goosely form. He noticed that he was crying uncontrollably. There was a strange silence within him. Gomer knew that he knew. Even though he was crying, he felt calm and reassured. He felt as though he were being cleansed and purified. At the depths of his soul, he could feel peace and tranquillity. The silence within him observed this whole process. This silent stillness was his true identity. It was peacefully watching his story unfold, yet it remained totally unattached.

Grandpa waited and watched, for he knew that Gomer had just taken a leap forward in the process of transformation. "You have finally admitted your personal powerlessness. You have finally admitted that you need our help and that of the Great Wing. The whole flock is here for you. And is there something else that you have realized?" asked the old goose with a smile.

"Yes," said Gomer. "I really do believe that there is a Great Wing thought within me. I know it. I know it because . . ." He started to falter.

Grandpa proceeded to explain further. "As you released your personal control, you were able to view yourself almost silently without the pain. You were in awe of the whole process from that place of peace within." The certainty in Grandpa's voice demonstrated to Gomer that he had understood what had happened.

"That's right," said the younger goose. "I seemed to know what was happening. My emotions had overwhelmed me, but I was somewhere deep inside, quietly watching the whole thing, as though I were in perfect harmony with all of Nature. I was the silent, eternal observer." At that moment there was a blast of cold wind, but this time he didn't even feel it. All he felt was peace.

Now he understood. His training must continue. He had made his decision.

8
Flight Training

Grandpa knew that Gomer was ready for flight training. "There is an interesting part of the flight training that we should discuss," Grandpa said. "You see, there is a phase in flight when you are at the peak and you allow the Great Wing to take over your mind." He paused to allow Gomer to absorb this idea. "What results is a curious form of relaxation and altered state of consciousness. The mind becomes exceptionally quiet, and you hear the words 'Great Wing, Great Wing' chanting slowly and evenly at the depths of your being. The conscious control of your mind has been released." Grandpa raised his brows a bit, for he knew that Gomer was skeptical. "Your free will has been released from the bonds of an ego that acts childishly and irrationally. Your inner self is in operation and your whole flight will be transformed into autoflight."

"Is that when the glow starts?" asked Gomer.

"Precisely," said Grandpa Goose. "It can be seen by anyone who maintains the Flock Mind. This is very important, because if you ever doubt that you have the Flock Mind, the glow is an awesome reminder that you are still maintaining it."

The old bird stopped and thought for a moment. "In any event, the lead bird starts to glow. His body fills with pure energy. His wings start to beat with an incredible force, and he transcends his own limitations. He is flying the potential of the whole flock formation. On a purely physical level, the lead bird has the combined strength of the whole flock. On a mental level, while the Great Wing thought keeps repeating itself, the lead bird can direct the whole flock with his thoughts." Grandpa appeared to be enjoying what he was saying, as if he were remembering the feeling.

"How can he do that?" asked Gomer, obviously in awe of his grandfather's tale.

"Well, the bird at the peak has to hold the visualization of the whole flock and its movement. He then thinks himself into the flock, as if it were one giant set of wings, and proceeds to guide them to their destination." Grandpa made it sound so simple and effortless. "When you function as if you were a giant set of wings, there is an intense love that you feel for your flock. You feel empathy and compassion for all the other birds. It is a wonderful feeling. You've heard about this, haven't you?" asked Grandpa.

"I remember what Gracious Goose once told me about holding loving thoughts of your fellow geese," said Gomer. "She said that if you hold loving thoughts about your fellow geese while you are at the head of the flock, you will experience absolute compassion. She also said that I would understand this completely only when I had reached the peak position and visualized the drop bird being picked up by the flock. What did she mean, Grandpa?" asked Gomer.

"Most geese think that the drop bird is out to catch the tail end of the greater wing and that he does it by himself," said Grandpa. "This is not exactly what happens. The drop bird has let go of the Great Wing thought and retreats into the Flock Mind. He starts to falter. He may be so exhausted that he feels his own weakness. The drop bird doesn't believe that he will be able to reattach himself to the flock. The lead bird must envision the drop bird catching the flock while the greater wing simply descends a little and attracts him back into the flock. The air currents around the flock allow for even the most tired and despondent bird to return to formation. Even if he experiences absolute weakness, he is retrieved. It is the lead bird who picks him up while maintaining the expression of the Great Wing."

Gomer started to understand what Grandpa was describing. "You mean that the drop bird doesn't catch the flock on his own?" he asked.

"Oh no," said Grandpa. "It may appear that way to the casual observer, but in reality the drop bird may not want to be taken in because he feels burned out. He may be feeling sorry for himself. He may be so fatigued that he is unable to think clearly about his flight patterns."

"Couldn't he just switch back to the Great Wing thought and continue?" asked Gomer.

"Not really," said Grandpa. "He is too concerned about having lost it momentarily and is very upset that he has dropped all the way down. I don't know if you can understand all of this," added Grandpa, "but after soaring so high and then losing the ideal, the bird becomes a little negative, and immediately there is a total reversal and he falls. When his attitude returns to the Flock Mind, he needs a period of time to recuperate from the physical changes he has experienced. He needs to rest in the draft of the greater wing."

Gomer was listening intently. "While he is in the greater wing, he will go through the various stages of maintaining the Flock Mind, and his position will rotate back up toward the peak. You see, this whole process has an order that reflects the overall needs of the flock and supports the individual needs of each bird. The drop bird will be back in full force relatively quickly because of the collective power of the whole flock. It is interesting to see how the size of the flock and its collective energy can make such a difference in the energy available to the individual bird," said Grandpa. "We'll take you through the stages to get to peak and allow you to experience it all."

"I'll get to practice it?" asked Gomer.

Grandpa smiled. "There really isn't any practice. It just seems as though there is always enough time for a few trial runs prior to the migration. Let me stress that there is no practice involved. In life, every flight is for real. Having a drop facing you, even when you think you have time to practice, can be a little dangerous."

"I'll take it seriously," said Gomer thoughtfully, "especially the part about holding the thought that the whole flock can retrieve me, if I allow it, during a drop."

Grandpa looked at Gomer, nodded his head, and said, "You are ready for Gracious Goose, Gomer. You are ready for Gracious Goose and the inventory of present values."

9

The Inventory of Values

*L*ooking as serene as ever, Gracious Goose approached Gomer and Grandpa. Gomer wondered how she maintained such composure. She began to speak. "You learn from what you teach, Gomer, so be extremely careful about what you say to others. I have come to teach you about the inventory of present values. It is essential that you know yourself, and you will know yourself by knowing and understanding your values—including both your strengths and your weaknesses. If you are able to recognize your strengths, you can connect with another who has compatible values and fly in strength. This, of course, is attained by the primary value of honesty. An honest bird can fly in formation only if he has identified and overcome his doubts. He must have total faith that the Great Wing will manifest itself with complete intensity. He must truly believe that even he will be able to fly at the peak. Releasing doubt and placing a high value on hope are essential to this ability to fly."

Gracious Goose paused for a moment. "There is another aspect of honesty that has to be considered before making the migration, and that is the admission by each bird that he cannot do it alone. We are all aware of this fact, but many of us struggle with the idea that our own willpower is simply not enough. We struggle with the thought that the seasons are changing and that we are powerless over that change. Many birds have had to face the feeling of powerlessness that their environment was going to change to such an extent that they wouldn't be able to survive. Some poor unfortunates stayed and tried to use their willpower to adapt to the winter, and they failed. Others of us admitted the inevitable truth and went with the migration. The admission was simply being honest and nothing more.

"I remember when I was very young and preparing to undertake my first flight. I was picked up at the very end of the training session and brought into formation by Minion. You've seen him, haven't you, Gomer?" asked Gracious.

"Yes," he quickly replied. "Everyone knows Minion. He is famous for his courage, willingness, and perseverance in the face of adversity."

"Well, Gomer," said Gracious Goose, "he wasn't always like that. He gave those values to me, and they became his finest qualities. You see, on my first flight, I was afraid to join the flock. I felt that I should stay behind and face the great cold alone. I would remain and eat what was left. I was going to rough it in the great freeze and take my chances." She paused. "I was unwilling to take the measures necessary to bring the Flock Mind into my consciousness. I guess I was afraid of the great flight. I had never had the discipline and the willpower that the other birds had in the previous migrations." She stopped and looked him squarely in the eye. "I was most afraid of taking my inventory. You see, Gomer, I wanted to be considered beautiful by everyone. It was such a superficial trap. I looked really glamorous, but I was all pain on the inside."

"Well, you certainly are famous for your good looks now," Gomer said shyly as he blushed.

She brushed aside his remark and went on. "I was in distress. I didn't like me. I feared acknowledging my strengths and weaknesses. I dreaded that I would not be able to tolerate or accept who or what I was. I was trying to adapt to someone else's ideal of perfection." She gazed at the water and spoke. "I spent days playing on the pond. I was trying to convince myself that I was everybody's friend, but I was completely alone. I didn't feel that I fit in anywhere at all. When I had the opportunity to do an inventory of my strengths, I lied about them. I boasted, 'I've got it all. I've got everything it takes.' And yet I knew that I was deceiving the others and, most importantly, myself."

Grandpa smiled at Gracious Goose. "I remember

the day it dawned on you that you didn't even have the honesty to admit that you weren't perfect. Like everyone else, you thought that admitting to a few strengths and weaknesses meant you were inadequate to the task," he said.

Now Gomer was listening intently. He began to feel as if they were talking to his inner mind. He began to trust them more and more. He felt the trust that came with shared experience.

Gracious spoke gently to Gomer. "It takes humility to be honest about your strengths. It takes courage to change your weaknesses into strengths or to associate with those who have the abilities you want. Honesty, humility, and courage—these are the three primary values."

She paused to let Gomer think for a moment. "So let me get back to Minion. I secretly believe that he has everything it takes to be the Grand Goose this migration. You see, Gomer, he taught me courage, willingness, and perseverance, and in the process of teaching me, he learned them as well—so well that he is now a living demonstration of these attributes."

She stopped and looked at both of them. Grandpa nodded to encourage her to go on. "I was afraid to trust," she admitted. "Heed this value, Gomer, because the ability to trust is essential in order to take inventory of yourself. If you don't take inventory, you don't fly with us. It's as simple as that.

"Back then, when I started to look at my values, I had it all backwards. I mistrusted Grandpa when he was trying to bring me through the inventory of values. I needed to know which values were strong and which ones were weak. My weaker values had to be bolstered by associating with birds whose matured strengths were the same as my underdeveloped ones. I just wasn't ready. I was convinced that I would be criticized and ridiculed. I feared that I would be forced to reveal all sorts of unpleasant details about myself. It was frightening."

"Most of all," said Grandpa, "you misunderstood what humility really was."

"How true!" She was now beaming with joy. "That was my breakthrough. I finally came to realize that I was equal to all the other birds and had the Great Wing essence within me, just as everyone else did. I was astonished at how loving and beautiful I felt when I was finally in touch with that truth."

"How did that happen?" asked Gomer, becoming increasingly curious. This process still seemed so strange to him.

"Well, I was sitting around watching the other birds in their practice flights. At that point, I was still claiming that I wasn't going to leave with them. Minion came by and asked if he could stay with me and tell me a little about himself. Since I was so afraid of the upcoming freeze, I didn't bother to listen at first, but I tried to be polite." She stopped and smiled. "Minion kept at it. He started telling me that he didn't believe he had the courage to make the flight his first time, but he did it anyway, in spite of his fear."

"He had learned the difference between fearlessness and courage," interrupted Grandpa. "Courage is action in spite of your fear because you desire to attain a given result."

"Stop lecturing, Grandpa," said Gracious. "You sound like Professor Goosenstein." They all laughed.

Gracious Goose returned to her story. "I told Minion that I was unwilling to fly, and he just looked at me and said, 'When I was unwilling to fly, it was because I was too proud to take stock of my strengths and weaknesses. I wanted to be known for my strength and my perfect flying abilities. I was reluctant to pay the price to learn autoflight and to relinquish my will. I elected to will myself into hyperflight voluntarily. I didn't want to release control of my flight to my inner instinctual nature and let go. But I learned the difference between being considered a hot-shot high flyer and the willingness to surrender, which released in me the ability to fly with the flock.'" She paused. "Seeing this great big goose smiling so gently at me and knowing how hard it must have been for him to let go of his tough-guy front just made me melt."

"Were you ready for the inventory at this point?" asked Gomer.

"Yes, because humiliation had become humility," said Gracious Goose. "I was no longer afraid to ask for help. I was ready to change my whole personality in order to fly with the likes of Minion, Grandpa, and the Grand Goose. I was ready to accept both my weaknesses and my strengths so I could fly in perfect harmony. I stopped holding grudges against those I thought had hurt me during my times of playing on the pond. I had thought that those who didn't think I was the sweetest, most adorable bird of the flock were being mean to me. I had became so obnoxious that I had offended others. I realized that what I really wanted was to feel connected with the whole flock."

"She was so cute, Gomer," said Grandpa. "She wanted to run around the flock apologizing to the rest of us for the way she had behaved."

"I remember that Minion always stood by me and helped me. He taught me the value of forgiveness, that forgiving is 'for giving' to the Great Wing identity within the other. I realized that we all had developed a sense of the Great Wing. At that point, I wanted to share it with other birds who were still experiencing doubts and fears. I went back to the pond to share what I had found, just as Minion had shared it with me." She paused for a moment.

"Strangely enough, as soon as I approached another bird, I had to start the whole process over again. I instinctively knew that I had to tell them about my inability to maintain the Flock Mind without the help of my colleagues and the Great Wing. I needed to reassess my strengths and weaknesses repeatedly. I had a tendency to become egotistical. I thought that I was a superior bird or the savior. This was all part of my weakness."

"So the secret," said Gomer thoughtfully, "is that whenever I want to fly in perfect harmony, I must do my inventory in the here and now. I need to see how I interact with my fellow birds in a realistic sense, by looking at my values."

Gracious Goose nodded in approval. "You must develop a certain understanding about the hierarchy of your values. You see, I have just told you about the values of honesty, hope, faith, courage, trust, willingness, humility, and perseverance. However, you must know which values are the highest in your personal inventory on which you will base your life. There are some birds who wish that courage could be their primary value. Others believe that honesty is more important. Some believe that the unselfish, loving service to other birds is the greatest value. Many contest that the primary value is spirituality and understanding the nature of the Great Wing within.

"Since each bird is a bit different from the others, it is important that you understand your own value hierarchy. I suggest that you adopt all these values, including those of perseverance, restitution, forgiveness, and humility. Make them your own, for at various stages in your life, the knowledge that you receive from them will be extremely important to you. Your inner being has these values at its core. Knowing this will help you make crucial decisions. You will respond to situations based on how clearly you understand your values. Sometimes you will make decisions that seem foolhardy to others but that are based on your love and willingness to serve. Know each value well, Gomer, and allow it to become a pillar of strength upon which you can rest. Your values will guide you in making decisions that will affect your life."

10

Moving Up the Greater Wing

"Grandpa, this all sounds like a lot of theory," Gomer said. "Up to now, I've never had to fly with more than just one other bird, and I still drafted fairly well. But if I flew with a group, we would all be in disarray." He sounded very serious. "I've never experienced this whole formation thing."

"I know, Gomer, and that is OK. Let me tell you what happens and how the greater wing forms."

Grandpa called over Grand Goose and Gracious Goose, and the three of them flapped their wings and glided off into a low-flight pattern. Gomer followed and joined them. They started flying in a diamond formation, which was easy. Grand Goose began to talk, and Gomer listened intently. "There is a series of stages you must achieve while flying in formation in the greater wing. The first stage is acknowledging your powerlessness to migrate alone. The second stage is understanding that you can trust the Great Wing to take care of you in the great migration. The third stage is recognizing that your own ego is placing a limit on how fast and how far you can fly. The Great Wing will help you transcend these limits. The fourth stage is recognizing the need to be in perfect harmony with everyone in the flock. The fifth stage is turning over all flight to the Great Wing and letting it happen. Then, when you find yourself at peak, you will see that what you visualize and feel for the whole flock will be done in unison. Let's take a better look at all these concepts."

He paused for a moment. "Gomer," he asked, "what represents power to you? What forces here, as you fly, represent power to you?"

Gomer thought for a while. "Minion is powerful. He is the strongest goose in the whole flock."

"That's good," said Grand Goose. "Let's see what else represents power."

"I think the wind is powerful," said Gomer, "especially the hot, southerly wind that sometimes brings in a squall during the late summer." He paused to think. "A thunderstorm is very powerful," he said. They were gliding and adjusting to the winds as they flew around the pond. They approached a quiet haven along the shore. There, they wouldn't be bothered by any of the other geese.

"I think the lightning and thunder that accompany the storm are powerful," said Gracious Goose.

The other geese agreed that this was indeed a very powerful form of energy.

Grand Goose turned to Grandpa and asked him for his idea of power. "A hurricane is the most powerful force that I've ever flown through," Grandpa said.

"That's a great example," said Grand Goose. "There is no storm as forceful as a hurricane. If one approaches us, we look for land and take cover. We dread hitting one while flying over water, for it is extremely dangerous."

"I can see how powerful these things are, but I don't get what this has to do with moving up in the greater wing or with my lessons in Flock Mind training," said Gomer.

"Well, Gomer, we are going to tap into a force far more powerful than lightning, thunder, the high winds of a squall, or even a hurricane. We are going to tap into the power of the Great Wing. It is the Great Wing's consciousness that has fashioned the movement of the wind, the changes in seasons, and the movement of everything in Nature. This power is so great that a thousand migrations with a thousand storms couldn't match it."

Grand Goose paused and looked at each of the other geese. "I really feel quite powerless when compared to this force," said Grand Goose. "And in a sense, I am powerless in comparison to the infinite power of the Great Wing. In order to make this migration, I must request the help of the power of the Great Wing as it works through me and my fellow birds. I know I can't do it alone." He paused. "Don't you agree?" Grand Goose looked first to Grandpa and then to Gracious Goose. They both nodded in agreement.

"How about you, Gomer? Without the Great Wing, are you powerless to make the great migration?"

"Yes, well, of course," he said. "I sure wish I understood this whole thing," he said in confusion. "I've decided that I can't do this thing all alone. I just hope I can get the nature of the Great Wing to fly through me and do whatever I can to survive this migration."

"Gomer, do you believe if you were the father of a pair of little geese and they wanted you to help them find just enough food for their next meal that you would help them?" asked Grand Goose.

"Well," said Gomer, "I would help them find food for as many meals as I could, and I would also help them develop the means to find it themselves. I would certainly think about what type of food they were going to eat and all the other things they would need, not just the one meal they were concerned about. Why do you ask?"

"Gomer, the Great Wing will provide you with whatever you need to survive this migration," said Grand Goose. "It will respond to you in a very personal way and give you far more than you ask for, even before you inquire. The Great Wing knows exactly what you need, but you must ask in order to start the flow. When you are in the point position and are visualizing for the whole flock, the Great Wing nature will cause the flock to follow whatever command you wish. The flight pattern of the whole flock will follow your thought. This leads me to the next step in attaining the Great Wing thought as you move up the greater wing." Grand Goose paused.

Grandpa took up the lesson. "You see, Gomer, the first two stages of acknowledging your personal powerlessness and understanding that you can trust the Great Wing to respond to you are the ones you must master first. You do this when you are on the end of the greater wing drafting us and while you are moving up. Then you will realize that your thoughts and feelings of being separate from the Great Wing and of not really being a part of it will cause you to have anxieties and fears. By this point, you become doubtful of leading at the peak."

"Gomer," asked Grand Goose, "are you ready to have your belief system altered to accept hyperflight and autoflight? If you are, your whole ability to fly will be transformed, and you will soar in ways that you never dreamed were possible."

"Is it necessary, every time, to affirm that your belief system will be altered?" asked Gomer.

Grand Goose looked at him intently. "Gomer . . ." He paused for a long while. "Gomer, while you are in the greater wing, you will need to have your belief system remain as flexible as the Great Wing requires it to be. This is so you can do whatever needs to be done. You cannot imagine all the wonderful things that can happen while flying at the peak, but you must remain open to all possibilities. Your ability to remain unbiased will expand your ability to perform." Grand Goose stopped and allowed Grandpa to talk.

"Another way of saying it is that the Great Wing will perform through you," said Grandpa Goose. "Your beliefs have always been the limiting factor of your performance."

Grandpa looked to Grand Goose, who appeared serene and tranquil, and then spoke slowly. "I had to turn my life over to the power of the Great Wing in order to fly with the whole flock." Gomer asked Grandpa and Gracious Goose in turn if they had turned their flight over to the control of the Great Wing. Grandpa added that he had also let go of his will and not just his false beliefs about his flying abilities.

"It's both the will and false beliefs that must be sacrificed, Gomer," said Gracious Goose. "Personal desires are released and replaced with the dedication to fly in flock formation and make it to peak."

"In other words, Gomer," asked Grand Goose, "are you willing to let yourself be changed at depth by the power of the Great Wing? Are you willing to let the Great Wing take over and support your flight?"

Gomer felt a little calmer now, almost as if this process were just a restatement of all the various teachings that he had learned during the summer.

Now he was a little more confident that he would be able to get the hang of this whole thing.

Grand Goose was talking again. "When you are at this stage of flight, you will be next to the point position, and while there, you will need to master the final stage before the point bird drops. The final and most important stage before flying at the peak is forgiveness. You must first forgive the mistakes of the birds that preceded you or caused you any harm. Make sure you hold no grudges against anyone, anyone at all in the entire flock. Do you understand?" Each of the birds nodded in agreement.

"Finally, you must forgive yourself and know that in spite of all your previous mistakes in flying, you are at the right place at the right time. You must know and believe that you can fly at peak."

Grand Goose turned to Grandpa. "First, have you forgiven every other bird that ever harmed you in any way?"

"I forgive everyone," said Grandpa, "and I know that they were doing the best they possibly could at the time." Gracious Goose agreed, and Gomer nodded his head also.

"Now let's forgive ourselves for anything we ever did that we may perceive as harmful to ourselves or that is not in keeping with our own values and expectations," said Grand Goose.

"I forgive," said Grandpa.

"Me too," said Gracious Goose.

Gomer thought for a while and said, "I even

forgive myself for not learning this whole hyperflight thing sooner."

"Let's go!" shouted Grand Goose, and he took off. The other three birds followed and fell into a line of four birds. Gomer started to go through the various things he had learned, and as he forgave himself, he watched the peak bird fall and realized that he was all the way up to the head of the line. He quickly took all four and went down to the pond.

"What's the matter?" asked Grand Goose.

"I didn't know what to do at the point," said Gomer.

"You simply turn your flight over to the Great Wing and then let it happen. You were doing fine," said Grandpa. "So we'll get on with it. You just thought your way down to the pond, and that's good."

Grand Goose was grinning and said, "Grandpa, he's just trying to intellectualize this whole thing. He believes he can use his mind to think it through." Gracious Goose and Grand Goose started to smile, said a quick good-bye, and then they took off, leaving Grandpa and Gomer alone on the west shore of the pond.

"Did I mess up just then? I thought we'd fly a lot longer."

"No, but you need more work."

"Oh, I did do badly," said Gomer with a moan.

"No, that was good," said Grandpa. "You're ready for the next part of your training. Because you intellectualized at the moment you did, you must spend the rest of the day with Professor Goosenstein."

11

Goosenstein

"I'm going to spend the day with Goosenstein? Oh, but he's so analytical, and he's always blaming people for whatever happens to them," said Gomer.

"He really isn't," said Grandpa. "He has some valuable insights that must be learned quickly. He is the right goose for you at this time." Gomer felt Grandpa's support as he spoke.

"Oh, Grandpa!" cried Gomer. "I trust you, but do I really have to spend time with him? What if I can't find him? He may be busy, you know. Suppose I can't understand him?" He noticed that Professor Goosenstein was approaching him from his right side and decided that his excuses were useless. As he drew closer, he started to laugh. "We were just speaking about you, Professor, and here you are!"

Goosenstein rumpled his feathers. "I didn't just

happen to be here, and you know that. And you weren't just speaking about me. You were thinking and feeling on the level of certainty, and you are ready for your training." The Professor started to smile, and Grandpa rumbled with laughter.

The Professor proceeded to speak to Gomer. "Do you know why some geese have so many problems with their flight? They think of uncontrolled loops and spins while they are trying to fly straight. Others think about flying fast when they want to fly slowly, and still others think about flying slowly when they want to fly fast. You will get pretty unpredictable results if you think left and then try to fly right."

Grandpa was watching and chuckling as the Professor rapidly stated one point after another.

"Aw, this is all too simple!" said Gomer Goose.

Goosenstein started to laugh and said, "Sure it's simple, and you're thinking complicated—complicated, when I'm teaching simplify. Simplify! Reduce!! Reduce!!! Everything has a common denominator, and it's the Great Wing. It runs through life and is the underlying unity of all creation. If you can realize that without complicating it too much, you'll understand what I'm trying to teach you." The Professor slowed down.

"At a certain point, I had to admit that my own thoughts were the controlling factor of my flight. I tried to analyze why I flew wrong or why I had to flap my wings a little extra, but the answer was always the same. My thought controlled the direction of my flight." He paused to allow Gomer to think about what he had said. "I blamed the wind, the rain, the updrafts, the downdrafts. I blamed anything I could. I would become afraid when I stalled in midair. I thought it was the wind and not my thoughts that were causing my problems. Finally, I had to upgrade my flight beliefs. My body and all these feathers," said the Professor, "know exactly what to do in order to get me to wherever I want to be, wherever I can think of being. The problem for me was that I couldn't think about where I wanted to go without frequently changing my mind."

Gomer pondered this. "I don't really believe that I can attain the Flock Mind. It's not that I can't think about where I want to go. I just don't believe I can achieve it."

"That's right, but wouldn't you like to?" asked the old Professor.

"Of course."

"Then it's yours if you expand your thinking to encompass the thought of the Flock Mind and keep your mind off what you don't want. Now, isn't that simple?"

The Professor continued with his lesson. "Your belief system interferes with your natural flying instinct." He waited for this to sink in. "Every year when the cold wind comes, there are many young birds who have thicker feathers, but they don't understand why. Instinct is the answer. They make all sorts of adaptations to what they are doing and go through the training as though it were the most simple transition in the world. Later, they are in awe of how grand Nature really is in this respect." The Professor seemed to be watching for Gomer's reaction. "Everything you need to make this transformation is supplied to you from within. All you have to do is ask for it and you will receive it. I remember when I was on my first flight. It was so scary and yet so much easier than I thought. You must recognize that you have limitations. These limitations are ones that you have placed on your own thinking. Now, listen closely, Gomer. These limitations are usually based on your current perceptions of your past experiences. These perceptions cloud what you are seeing right now."

"Wait a minute! What is a perception of a past experience?"asked Gomer.

"I'm glad you asked," said Professor Goosenstein. "You probably believe that your flight is limited by what you actually learned and experienced in your previous flights, which is close to but not quite the truth. Your view of past experiences may be very distorted. Certain perceptions of the past affect how an experience will limit your life, but it is never the past experience per se that is limiting."

"What do I need to do to change the way I believe?" Gomer asked, following the Professor's wisdom for the moment.

"Well, you could start by letting go of your belief in limitations. When you are at the peak of the flock, you have unlimited thinking, and anything is possible. When you let go of limiting beliefs, your whole life will be transformed, and I mean *all* of it—the past, the present, and the future!"

"How can I transform the past and the future?" asked Gomer. "The past has already happened and the future has not, so I don't see how I can have much control." Gomer thought he had logically tripped up the Professor.

"You restructure the past by changing what you do with your memories. For instance, take a look at a painful memory from your past. Look at the whole sequence of images as they actually happened. If you run that sequence backwards quickly, you will reduce or eliminate the pain. If you reinterpret the meaning of a past event, your emotions about it will change. In the same manner, your perception of the future is created by your thinking about it. It is important not to limit your thinking about the future. Ultimately, your thinking about the past and the future is acting like a filter on the present. Get control of the now, by letting go of the past and the future, and you have control of all time for all times." Gomer could now see that Goosenstein had been through this before.

There was a long pause. Gomer couldn't believe what he had just heard. His whole life—past, present, and future—would be altered if he simply concentrated on controlling his thoughts in the now. Gomer gathered all of this in his mind and asked,

"All I have to do is remember to be here now and then some sort of transformation will take place?"

"Yes, a transformation that is quite astounding. It takes place on the level of thought, yet for all intents and purposes, the average goose would swear that it occurred on the level of physical reality. Remember that in flying you think where you want to go first and then fulfill the desire by releasing this thought on the most subtle level of consciousness," said Goosenstein. "You must think it into existence for yourself, but think it by releasing your limits on flying."

Goosenstein's voice became very gentle and soft. "It is imperative that you surrender your flight to the Great Wing and allow what you are doing to change you at depth. Without complete release of all disturbing thoughts, you will be unable to maintain the Flock Mind. You see, Gomer, there comes a time during the great flight when flying becomes automatic and remains that way. To reach this state, you must gradually build up your concentration as you step up from the last bird to the point position. You really get into a flow during the flight. Each position is an opportunity to intensify the Flock Thought in your mind until finally you realize that you are one with the Great Wing and are in the peak, floating effortlessly. We call this ultimate position *autoflight*," he said. "It is so peaceful and serene, yet to an observer, it looks as though you are exerting more energy than you have the potential for. An ordinary goose during an ordinary time would become fatigued just watching you. You'll have the opportunity to experience this soon enough, so let's get on with the lesson."

The Professor smoothed his feathers momentarily. "There is a lesser and a greater wing of the great formation. You know that the left side is the wing of lesser length. It must be of lesser length or the formation cannot fly. The lesser wing is manned both by the older, infirm birds and by those who understand the need for migration but don't yet have the ability to work the greater wing.

"You will be flying the greater wing. The major difference between the two wings is that the birds of the greater wing rotate. The last bird of the greater wing slowly moves up the line until he is the lead bird. The greater wing is the power wing and is drafted by the lesser wing in much the same way as the rear bird is drafted by the one in front of him."

"Why is it, then, that not everyone wants to go through this transformation?" Gomer asked the Professor.

"Everyone has an excuse that they use for different situations. Once a goose has invested enough time in developing an excuse, he will use it over and over again in all sorts of predicaments. Our thoughts are like our children. They are created in and through us. Sometimes we defend them, even though we really know that they are wrong. We hate to give up the things we've created or even correct the things we've created in error."

Grandpa cleared his throat and said, "So making excuses can actually be quite efficient; if I say that I'm too old, or too young, or that I like where I am, I've got the same excuse for at least five or six different situations."

"I'd like to get rid of my excuses," said Gomer.

"Sometimes it's helpful to look at them and laugh," said Grandpa. "You'll benefit when you hear someone using an excuse that is obviously silly or illogical and can help him overcome that excuse. It is also helpful to observe one goose help another with a very serious excuse."

12
Bette and Her Mate, August

"Grandpa, I think that Gomer is ready to watch Walter help Bette. She's been having a terrible time for the past few days," said the Professor. Walter often counseled birds who were in turmoil over the migration but had migrated before. He especially liked to help couples in distress recognize that they had to take care of themselves individually before the migration and not focus so much on fixing their mate or helping their mate get ready.

Bette was talking with her friend Walter. Her demeanor was a little different than usual, and it appeared that she was upset. She was looking down and nodding her head slowly. Walter was saying something she apparently agreed with but did not want to accept. She raised her voice and Gomer could hear her saying, "But I know that already! I just can't get myself to leave August behind. I love him! He's my mate and he means so much to me!"

Walter stood up straight, smiled, and said, "I know. I understand. We all love him. If he refuses to make the flight, we can't force him. We will do whatever we can, but ultimately he'll have to think the Flock Thought on his own or he'll be left behind. Now listen and please hear me. If you tell him that you will stay behind to help him, he will never join in to fly in flock formation. You must pull away from him so he can learn on his own."

"But I love him!" she protested.

Walter became stern. "Has your love taught him to fly? Has your willingness to stay by him, if he chooses to remain, helped him get his thoughts into harmony? Of course not." Bette was silent as Walter spoke. "So now is the time to stop. Let us work with him and let him know that you will be here in the formation if he wants to join us. Tell him that since you are his mate for life you expect him to get it together and won't accept less from him, period."

Then Walter noticed Gomer and motioned for him to come over. He spoke to her again. "The real reason you need to reconsider staying behind is for you. There is no hope of anything good being gained by supporting your mate in his weakness. You will be the one to suffer immeasurable pain and misery."

He turned to the younger goose. "Gomer, you're new to the Flock Mind teaching, and you understand the need to create density, so I don't need to explain that. We can proceed. Normally, our friend Bette would be getting ready to fly with us, but August, her mate for life, has decided to stay behind and play in the pond. She believes that she can stay behind with him to help him in case the winter gets too rough." Walter then paused and looked at Bette with urgency. "It will be difficult, even fatal, to do so. The great cold is lethal to a goose. The geese who stayed behind thought, 'I can handle it. I'll experience just a little of its fury and then leave.' But there may be no one around when you want to leave. They always say the same thing: 'I can handle it. Others couldn't, but a little cold won't bother me—I'm tough!'"

He was now talking to Gomer directly. "And they never make it. It gets colder and colder. When the winds come, the water freezes and the lake gets covered with ice, which is not exactly paradise for a goose."

Gomer wondered if Bette would make it. He then remembered what Grandpa had said: "Look and see if the goose has a mate. They almost always fly together. Almost invariably they make it, if one of the pair is willing to surrender to the Great Wing essence within. They may not make it to Flock Mind at the same time, but since they are a pair, they will go together. There is a strange thing about geese that are paired. They have a special bond that always keeps them together, and they remain mates for life, even if along the way they possess an attraction for another bird. This particular bond is rarely found in the animal kingdom. It is one of the noble forces that separate geese from other animals. This special force unites these geese, and it also powers the lead bird in the greater wing."

Gomer had been staring at Bette. She noticed the funny look on his face. She felt as though he wanted to ask her something. She acknowledged his quizzical look with a nod. "Are you and August mates for life?" he asked.

She started to cry, confirming his thought. He knew that they would stay together and continue on the course they had chosen. Bette would be a little late in reaching the Flock Mind consciousness because of her emotional attachment to August. She needed to let go of him so that her belief system would not be contaminated by his. For the sake of her growth, she needed to stop helping August. It's one thing to offer him help, but it's another to make it easier for him to shirk his responsibilities and goof off.

As she continued to cry, Walter gestured for Gomer to go back to Grandfather Goose. Watching Bette struggle, Gomer realized that there was no excuse for not making the transformation. Only his own fear and confusion stood in his way. He had relinquished his excuses, and now he was ready for whatever would come next. He spotted Grandpa motioning to him over by the shore of the pond.

13

Holding the Flock Mind

Returning to the pond, Gomer asked, "Grandpa, who is the best one to talk to about how to hold the Flock Mind thought while in the greater wing?"

"Well, you really can't discuss this with just one bird. You need to speak with your Uncle Ernest and his mate, Monica. They are the perfect pair for you to listen to," said Grandpa.

Gomer swam over to the south shore of the lake. On the way, he thought about this odd pair. They were hardly around during the summer. They always flew together and seemed to be involved mostly in their own specific tasks, yet they were always part of the great migration. They were wingmates for life.

He remembered when he had first heard about the idea of wingmates. Grandpa had told him how only geese have the capability of staying mates for life, although they don't always do it. When they do, they must be willing to put up with great hardship and also great joy. He wanted to ask Monica and Ernest about being wingmates. He also wanted to ask them about thought concentration with this Flock Mind thing.

Actually, Gomer was a little confused about the Flock Mind. He had thought for sure that he would learn about this mental technique from Professor Goosenstein. Surely the Professor, with his enormous intellectual talents and his discipline, would have been the bird to learn from.

Instead, he was going to visit the old lovebirds. Was there some sort of secret that they possessed about the mind, or had Grandpa been a little off-base this time? He was eager to find out, so he swam faster. He could see them on the other side of the pond, lazily frolicking around. They didn't seem to be as busy as the others were, and they looked a bit too relaxed to be helping the flock reach Density One.

As Gomer approached, Ernest looked at him humorously and asked him if he would like to fish or think about the Flock Mind.

Monica stopped and looked at him. "Think Flock Mind, and let's go fishing!" Then, with very little hesitation, she rambled on, "No, wait, the Flock Mind. No, maybe we can look for food on the shore. No, I think I'll think about the Flock Mind."

"Oh no!" thought Gomer. "She's a scatterbrain! I've come over here trying to find out about Flock-mindedness, and she can't decide what she wants to do. I would also like to go fishing and not have to worry about Density One."

Just then Monica turned to Ernest. "The Flock Mind, Ernest."

"Yes, I know, but I keep losing it, and I'm not so sure what I'm going to do about it," he confessed.

"Just think it, and then go fishing or something," she said.

"I just don't know," Ernest said. He then noticed Gomer and asked, "Is there something you want to talk to me about, or do you want to hang out and play?"

"Oh, gosh," he thought. "This is *so* unstructured. I don't think I should bother." He turned and walked away.

"Stop, Gomer," Ernest said. "We can help you, but you have to maintain the Flock Thought so we can get to Density One. We sure would like to start the migration, but we can't yet, because there aren't enough birds thinking the Flock Thought."

"So what do you think—can we do it?" Monica asked.

Now Gomer was really frustrated. He not only didn't understand them, but he didn't even believe they were capable of teaching a structured lesson. He composed himself. "There are a few important questions that I would like answered."

They both turned in unison to face Gomer and encouraged him to proceed. He found himself noticing how much alike they looked, and he remembered what Grandpa had said: "When a goose lives with another goose for a long time, they start to resemble each other because their thoughts have come into harmony. The more perfect the harmony, the greater the synergy, and after many years, the physical characteristics eventually change."

"Your first question?" she asked.

Gomer quickly rattled off his questions. "Is holding the Flock Thought an intellectual or feeling task? Do I have to think it in my mind or feel it in my gut? Do I think the words 'Flock Mind' or try to feel what it's like to be a part of the flock in flight?"

"That's three questions in one," said Monica. "I think we can give you only one answer, don't you, Ernest?"

"Surely, Monica. One good answer to three good questions," said Ernest.

She then gave her answer: "You have to think and feel at the same time in order to get the full depth and meaning of the flock into your mind."

"When both the beak and the gizzard are in harmony," Ernest laughed, "you've got the Flock Thought in place. You must be able to hold the proper thoughts in your mind, even while you are performing the most mundane behaviors. You see, Gomer, your whole organism must be in tune with the flock consciousness, and your whole being must be able to respond."

"Your feelings must be in harmony with your thoughts. No harmony, no results," Monica said.

"How do I know when my thoughts and feelings are in harmony?" asked Gomer, still puzzled.

"That's another very good question, Gomer," said Ernest. "Monica, my dear, why don't you tell him, using the level of feelings?"

"I would surely love to help him grasp the essence of this idea, Ernest, so let me start. You will be able to understand the full meaning of these words when you allow your beliefs about who you really are to turn around." She hesitated and looked at Ernest, then back to Gomer.

"You are not your goose body and all the sensations attached to it. You are not your goosely thoughts and all the ideas that float through your mind as you talk to yourself. You are not your goosely feelings. Finally, you are not all the strange moods and excited states that you experience as you fly through the air and perform all your wondrous aeronautical feats. You are not any of these, and yet you are. You are the silent observer within of your body, thoughts, and feelings. You are part of the great flock that forms each migration. You will be what you are, because you are made in the image of the Great Wing's essence. The Great Wing has always been the foundation of your being. Even in your hour of ignorance and doubt, when you are filled with fear and anxiety, you will always remain you—not the little Gomer, learning how to fly and searching after the truth of the Great Wing and the Flock Mind, but rather the Great Wing itself. Its essence and instinctual nature are who you are. As a goose, you have the ability to be whatever the Great Wing can see for you. You must turn your life over to the care and guidance of the Great Wing within and let it bring you to the fulfillment of your purpose."

"Sometimes," said Ernest, "your thoughts and feelings will take you on long internal flights through great storms. You have not flown even an inch and yet the Great Wing has used this internal flight time to train you, to polish you, and to form you into a more perfect expression of the Great Wing. Sometimes it is distorted by the lesser side of your personality, but even when you are fishing, you will always be expressing the greater side that exists within you. You are not the act of fishing or the fisherman. You are the observer who silently watches and acknowledges the beauty of all things in Nature."

"Now, do you want to go fishing or talk about the Flock Mind?" asked Monica.

Suddenly Gomer understood—not only by his intellect or only by his feelings, but by both, simultaneously. He realized that the nature of the Great Wing was indeed in all birds and that when the time for the long flight was upon him, he would know. He knew that all was right and that all things occur in their appropriate times. He was experiencing an incredible bliss. He was peaceful and serene.

Just then, an icy blast of wind broke his thought. He heard Grandpa's voice traveling along the cold current. "Density has been achieved! Let's go!"

14
The Long Trip Begins

Gomer heard Grandpa yell again, "Let's go!" He could see the other eleven neighboring flocks already in the air. Now was the moment of destiny, the time for Gomer and his colleagues to apply what they knew and take to the air.

The past few days of learning the hyperflight phenomenon had been exhilarating, but there was an urgency in his grandfather's voice, and he knew it was time. Grand Goose was circling around, and he was waiting for Minion and Gracious Goose to join in next.

Minion was flying slowly over the pond, and Gracious followed, also flying ever so slowly. At a certain point, Minion started to accelerate, and his lady kept the pace right behind him. They didn't miss a beat. Gomer watched Grand Goose kick up the speed at which he was flying, which he did all by himself. It was awesome. His power and beauty flashed across the morning sky. His great wings beat with intensity. Gomer now understood a little more about the Grand Goose and his responsibility to the flock. Grand Goose was going to hit hyperflight alone and then shift into autoflight in time for Minion and Gracious Goose to come from behind and draft. At that precise moment, the three of them would be in formation, and the migration would begin.

He watched excitedly as the two geese raced in a circle, slowly changing the shape and direction of their arc. On the first pass, they were not close enough to Grand Goose, but you could see Minion starting to chant while adjusting his speed and direction.

On the second pass, they got closer. Their arcs were a little more in line as they flew at different speeds and at slightly different altitudes.

On the third pass, they raced together. In Gomer's eyes, this was the most beautiful sight he had ever seen. Their speed seemed to have synchronized about halfway back to their rendezvous point. Grand Goose started to bank slightly, and at the same time Minion shifted his wings from side to side. Their wings were beating in unison as they raced even closer toward each other.

They swung around in a combined arc with Grand Goose only a few yards ahead. The pair behind was gaining ground with every beat of their wings. Grand Goose started to glow. It was magnificent! Gomer could see it. He could actually see the glow!

They inched a little closer together. Minion

seemed to move down ever so slightly, and then he faltered. At that precise moment, Gracious Goose moved right into her place behind Grand Goose. Minion was falling a little farther behind when the two birds in front slowed their pace and dropped their altitude. Gracious Goose almost descended upon Minion, and when she moved close enough, his wings started to beat in harmony with hers.

There was a slight delay in wing movement from one bird to the next, which appeared like a gentle ripple moving from the first bird to the next.

Gomer was in awe of the whole process, and then he was a little startled to see Grandpa take off with tremendous honks and powerful wing beats. He watched him climb slowly into the air, banking and gliding, and then he climbed some more. Grandpa swung around and motioned for Gomer to take to the air. Gomer could feel his heart racing as he started to flap his wings and make some noise. He started to move forward, but then he realized that he needed to think the Flock Thought and look at Grand Goose. He felt the powerlessness and frustration of too many techniques and information overwhelming him. He let go, just to fly for a few seconds and feel the wind. Then Gomer caught the knowing eye of Grandfather Goose, who was just ahead of him. Gomer quickly brought his body right up behind the older bird.

"So far, so good," Gomer thought. His momentary sense of accomplishment persuaded him to concentrate. "Now let me think about the Flock Mind and see what happens." He felt a slight intoxicating rush of energy and noticed that he was beating his wings somewhat harder. He could see that the pace was picking up and that Grandpa was pulling him. The pace shifted again and they were in hyperflight. The two birds completed the first arc.

"Flock yes," he found himself thinking as the three other birds breezed by. Down below him, he noticed that Goosenstein and Bill had started racing toward them in their arc.

They completed the second pass. Gomer could see Grand Goose as the glow intensified. His wings shifted as they hit the side of Minion's draft. All five birds gently shifted, and Grandpa swung around again. Beneath them, Ernest and Monica took to the air.

They completed the third pass. Suddenly it happened. Grandpa went right under Minion, faltered, and left Gomer directly in the draft. He had made it into the greater wing! He had been picked up and now he was in. As a result of his sound training, and despite all his fears of not being able to do it, Gomer had made it. He felt as if he were not really beating his wings at all.

"Easy," he thought. "This is incredible!" He realized that he was drifting down over Grandpa and that his position was changing ever so slightly, without any effort. Grand Goose moved the greater wing right over Grandpa, and the draft picked him up.

They circled around again. Now Ernest and Monica approached them while Walter and Bette took to the air. Goosenstein swung around, completed his third pass, and placed Bill directly into Grandpa's draft. Ernest and Monica followed suit as Walter neared at a slower speed.

It seemed that Bette was having her doubts. Gomer noticed that August hadn't taken to the air with any of the flocks and was still swimming in the pond, playing like a fool. He was acting calm, cool, and collected, as if nothing were bothering him, and his pretense made him look out of place. He was clearly in a panic and in pain.

Just then, Gomer noticed that some older birds had formed the lesser wing and were encouraging August to join them. "Go ahead and join them," he thought. "So what if it turns out that you make this flight on the lesser wing? Just get going! You've got the potential to fly the peak, but that doesn't matter. Just join us!"

He saw that Bette and Walter were in hyperflight and performing pass number one. The lesser wing, not yet in hyperflight, started to close in at an angle. August was still down below, but now he wasn't playing. He was paddling around very slowly on the water, looking up for a few brief seconds and then quickly down again.

Walter passed the second time, and the greater wing shifted as it sped around. On the third pass, Bette joined in and Walter was picked up. Suddenly the whole wing started to slow down in unison in order to swing around and pick up the lesser wing.

15

The Practice Swings

The flock swung around the lake and made its first pass. The final formation revealed itself to the whole flock. Each bird was able to see the flock as a unity, but none so clearly as the bird in the point position.

They would have some practice sessions in which there would be a few drops for just the first three or four passes. They would then begin the flight and journey south for a few days. It would be a continuous flight, from dawn to dusk. They would fly great distances—more than one thousand miles! Gomer was excited. His mind raced as thoughts of the flight flashed before him.

"Flock yes," he could hear his mind repeating, as he realized that his position had moved up in the wing and that Grand Goose had dropped. Now Gracious Goose was maneuvering the whole flock.

He thought to himself, "Completely surrender to the fact that the flock flies together in order to survive. Flock yes." He realized that Gracious Goose had dropped and that now Minion was directing the flock to pick her up. He realized that he knew that the Great Wing was working through Minion and every bird in the flock.

"Flock yes." His thoughts did create his ability to fly. He was in love with the whole flock and was at peace. He realized that everyone was in the perfect place at the perfect time. There was order and peace.

Then Minion dropped and Gomer started the Great Wing chant in his mind. He was sure he could do it. He felt a surge of strength as he moved into peak. In his mind, he saw the whole flock descend a bit. The end of the greater wing inched down to pick up his powerful colleague.

"Great Wing," he heard at the depths of his being. He could see Minion becoming the Grand Goose, and he could also see a terrible storm. In his mind's eye, the Grand Goose was taking the whole flock through a dangerous wide arc. He shuddered as the thought reached his consciousness. He then felt a blast of cold wind and shivered. He had let go of the Great Wing thought and was falling. It was sickening. He couldn't believe the contrast. He grew somewhat tired and started to panic because he felt that he wouldn't be able to make it to the back of the wing. Just then, he saw that Grandpa was glowing. He felt the wind shift and caught the draft of the last bird.

Actually, Grandpa had maneuvered the greater wing right down on top of Gomer to pick him up. Then Grandpa dropped, followed by Bill and Professor Goosenstein, Bette, Walter, Ernest, and Monica. They each dropped in succession and moved up into their positions after the first drop was done.

They swung around the lake in a wide arc. He could see August, slowly paddling around the lake, beak down and looking obviously dejected. Then he heard Grandpa honking at him, reminding him to concentrate on the flock. Gomer forgave August in his mind and forgave himself for not concentrating. He shifted into the Great Wing thought just as Minion dropped, and a surge of energy hit him again. "Great Wing." He thought about all of his friends in the flock and moved the flock around. He could feel his ability to maneuver grow with each thought. "Great Wing." He could see Grand Goose flying alone at hyperflight, waiting for Minion to bring Gracious Goose in as the migration started. "Great Wing." As the lead bird at the peak, he could see the whole flock with him. Again he heard his grandfather honk. He then realized that he needed to drop at will for practice. He dropped, and it wasn't quite as bad as the first time.

He was easily picked up by Grandfather Goose. As the flock raced around again to make a third pass, the birds quickly shifted position to pick up speed.

The arc was even greater now, and the speed, though rapid, was easy to maintain. His thoughts returned to August and Bette, and he felt a tremendous compassion for the whole flock. Again the Great Wing chant stirred within him, and he moved up to the point position. With great ease, he picked up Minion and looked down. They were approaching his old friend August, perhaps for the last time. "Great Wing." He could hear the sound as it passed through his consciousness. "Great Wing." Suddenly he saw a picture of himself pleading with August to join the flock. Gomer noticed August performing all sorts of bizarre movements in the water. He faltered and started to drop. He knew what he had to do and fought frantically to fly toward his friend. Grandpa slowed the flock down in order to pick him up. Gomer then flew faster toward August. He knew what he had to do. Surely Grandpa wouldn't abandon him if he could just get August to take off with them. He had seen August move when he thought about him and knew that August had the Flock Thought in his consciousness. He knew that he could bring him in, if August would only get started.

The flock swung away and started to form a big circle. Grandpa dropped. They were going to make the wide arc again and were shifting positions. He could still see the lead bird glow and was confident that he would be picked up.

"August," he cried, "you can see the glow, can't you?" He was yelling excitedly as he approached his friend. "You can see the glow, can't you?"

August looked, nodded, and started to move.

Bette was the lead bird, and they both sensed that her love for them was very strong. They both knew it was a do-or-die situation. Gomer started to honk wildly to get his friend to act.

He intensified his honking while checking the flock's location. He could see Bette glowing splendidly. "Look at her, August. She's glowing! You can see it! Start moving! Flap your wings! Just do something! You'll see, it'll happen! Please get going!" Gomer was desperate.

August started to move, and in a few, terribly long seconds, he rose up into the air. They looked up just in time to see Bette drop. Walter swung the flock away a little, but they could still see the glow. Walter dropped, and the greater wing moved down to pick him up. Ernest was the next lead bird, then Monica. Then it was Grand Goose's turn. He swung the whole flock around toward the two struggling birds.

Gomer wondered where he would wind up but then realized that it didn't really matter. "Just keep your eyes on Grand Goose," he thought. And he saw the great old bird approaching the two younger birds. Grand Goose dropped and picked up the tail as they made their first pass, but Bill didn't quite maneuver them in. Bill dropped, which put the Professor in the lead. Gomer checked on August to see how his friend was doing. August was right behind him. Gomer picked up speed with a few fast beats of his wings. He checked again and August was right in his draft.

Gracious Goose took over the lead, and they raced away. It seemed that she wanted to let Minion pick them up. Again Gomer thought how magnificent Minion was. In his mind's eye, he could see him in the lead, with a great storm unleashing its furious wind on the flock. Minion dropped and quickly caught the draft. Both August and Gomer saw Grandpa glowing majestically. Grandpa had picked him up before, so he would do it again. He started to relax. The two birds' speed picked up as the flock swung in.

Gomer suddenly realized that he would have to drop and let August in first. He didn't know how to do it, so he panicked and faltered. As he faltered, August went sailing by and caught Minion's draft. Grandfather Goose gently allowed the tail of the greater wing to descend while he slowed down the flock to pick up Gomer. Gomer was back in. Now the migration could continue.

16
The Great Storm

The flock had been flying for days. The experience had been thrilling. Everyone, including August, seemed to have been able to handle the point position with power, grace, and ease. The Great Wing was bringing the flock to Chesapeake Bay without the slightest problem. Although there had been a few small storms, Grand Goose had grounded the flock during them. It had been quite easy and had caused no major disruption.

Gomer was enjoying himself immeasurably. He was particularly grateful that August and Bette had been able to fly together. They were both happy and wanted to continue on to their winter home promptly. He was very pleased with himself. Gomer grew tired after each drop he endured, so he too wished to settle at the winter home without delay. His mind went back to the lessons he had learned on the pond and at the summer bay. Now he knew what they were talking about when they had told him that being a dropped bird can cause all sorts of panic. He was feeling it with each drop. Now that the fatigue of the great flight had set in and was almost over, he felt that he understood the teachings better than ever.

"Sometimes the dropped bird has a feeling of desperation," he found himself thinking as he moved the greater wing downward to pick up August. It was quite an experience for Gomer to fly at peak and pick up his old friend. But he didn't like the idea of dropping, even though he still did it with ease. He felt such compassion for his friend August now as the greater wing picked him up.

The Great Wing chant was within him, and he experienced an incredible uplift of energy as he allowed his body to move in harmony with the thought. He felt transformed and knew that his fellow birds could see the glow as he traveled out at the point. It was a beautiful day, and he sailed along on winds of tranquillity.

Since there hadn't been a great tempest, he wondered if the title of the Grand Goose would remain the same this year. Grand Goose had kept his place in the lead position throughout the few small storms they experienced. Gomer's energy was peaking as he thought about Grand Goose. He could visualize him now, clearly in the lead, as a monster of a storm battered him while he pulled the whole flock safely through. As Gomer thought about the storm, his wings were beating with such power that the whole flock was moving faster than the usual hyperflight speed they had been maintaining. He thought to himself, "This is great. We'll get to our winter home even faster now!"

After he stayed in the point position and pulled the flock through the air, he went back in his mind to Grand Goose and his lectures. The Great Wing chant echoed as images of the lectures flashed through his mind.

"Every now and then, a great one comes to us." He could hear Grand Goose's voice. "In a terrible storm, all the other flocks join us and fly in unison with one 'V' inside the other. This has happened only a few times in the history of our migrations. It has invariably saved many birds and many smaller flocks."

Gomer was again feeling empowered and saw Grand Goose leading twelve flocks in a giant formation through a tremendous storm. It was a spectacular sight. His whole mind was filled with this scene as the Great Wing chant filled his consciousness.

As he thought to ask Grand Goose if that was how the last migration went, he noticed other flocks in the vicinity of his airspace. He became a little nervous and then he dropped.

His fall was somehow more sickening than he had anticipated, and his experience of despair was greater than he had imagined. Just then, in a frenzy of piteous flapping, he saw Grandfather Goose glowing. He also realized that the birds of the greater wing were getting ready to accommodate him back into the formation.

Gomer saw the other flocks in formation nearby and decided that he would ask how far they all were from the winter bay. "Maybe," he thought, "we are getting closer and we will soon be home. Could it be that the migration is really coming to an end?"

He began to calculate the distance mentally. "Let's see, for the last hundred miles or so we've been flying over water and marshland." And if he remembered correctly, the final forty miles of the migration would be all ocean. That seemed fairly simple, or was it? Hadn't he heard that there was something special about the last forty miles? But what? Gomer knew that now was not the time to try to recall his classes. He had to ask around. Surely someone would be able to tell him about the end of the journey. "Please tell me about the last hundred miles of the great migration," he found himself asking.

Grandpa looked at him, nodded, and explained. "The last hundred miles is a very special time. All the other flocks in our vicinity are also flying in the great migration, and then they proceed to approach each other. This is done so that we can fly in a giant formation, one flock inside the other, and land in unison at our winter home. It is a special time because the power of the Great Wing is heightend by the number of birds maintaining the Flock Mind. Gomer, it is an extraordinary time. The last forty miles or so are over open ocean. You will be enthralled by the experience of flying together, and your excitement will be powered by the enthusiasm that we all will generate. The Great Wing will lead us to the end of our migration. Once we are flying over the marshland, we will just about be able to see Chesapeake Bay. At that point, we are all together. We join in and form that special giant formation."

Gomer thought about this for a while. "Shouldn't we all feel very exhausted going the last forty miles? Shouldn't we all feel very tired?"

"Indeed," Grandpa said, "we will all be very tired. Physically, our bodies have been racked by the experience of the migration. We are all thinner. We are all weaker. We have been under tremendous stress for the last few days. However, the Great Wing essence has intensified, and the overall power of the flock will be greater than ever."

They were approaching the marshland now. They could see the long, flat, swampy field that heralded the last forty miles of open waters.

Gomer was able to move up the greater wing with ease. It was second nature for him to go through the transformation process now. It was the same for all of the birds that flew in this migration. They were able to move up the greater wing and transform from being a mere goose to the full expression of the Great Wing within. Through this natural process, each one became the point bird. Gomer Goose now understood what Grandfather Goose meant when he said that the process becomes natural to you. Instead of wondering how you can possibly achieve it, you now know that this is the way it's done.

Gomer again found himself at the point position. He felt alive. He felt strong. He felt empowered by the Great Wing. He was experiencing great surges of energy that he knew were not of his own making. He now knew his own powerlessness. They were all powerless but didn't appreciate it until they felt the power of the Great Wing. Until they felt the Great Wing's awesome potency, they believed that their personal power was a force to be reckoned with. But the power of the Great Wing was so huge in contrast to that of the individual goose that they came to understand their relative powerlessness. The Great Wing was far stronger than any storm they could face and far greater than the total power of the birds of the flock. It was the very strength of all of Nature itself.

He was now thinking of the landing at Chesapeake Bay. In his mind, he saw all the flocks flying together in the giant "V." He could see himself leading the flock down. What a tremendous thought! He then realized that it was time to drop. He let himself fall from the peak, and he did so with ease. Now it was much easier and smoother. This time, he dropped with grace and control. As he fluttered downward, he watched Grandpa glow majestically and was then gently picked up by the greater wing.

As he was picked up, he thought he noticed something gray on the horizon, which piqued his curiosity. He asked August if he knew what it was.

"Well, I sure hope it isn't a storm, Gomer," said August. "We've had enough storms during this migration. Those two so-called small ones were sufficient. Every time I think about a storm, I see myself at peak and then falling off in the storm. I just dread the idea of having to go through another storm." August was rambling on and starting to become negative. Gomer decided that he would not tolerate any negativity, so he quickly stopped August.

"Listen, August, the Flock Mind is where your mind needs to be. Let's just stay in formation. The flight is almost over, and I'm sorry I asked about it." But Gomer kept watching in the distance, and he was beginning to believe that it really was a storm. He could see it blowing in from the ocean. He pondered the idea of reaching Chesapeake Bay before the storm hit. There were many questions on his mind as he slowly moved up the greater wing. He was also wondering, if it were a storm and if it were to hit, who would be the lead bird. He could easily picture either Grand Goose or Minion in the point position. As he flew, he tried to imagine a way to stay in the point position long enough to ensure that if and when the storm hit, Grand Goose or Minion would be the lead bird.

The flock flew on. Now the twelve flocks were beginning to converge. They were such a beautiful and majestic sight! As they flew the last hundred miles toward their winter home, Gomer felt the greater wing gently pick up Grandpa. He paused and asked

Grandpa, "Is that a storm? Do I have to worry about this? A storm, Grandpa, right at the end of the whole migration? Maybe it's just some dark clouds, hey, Grandpa?"

Grandpa spoke calmly, "Think about the Flock Mind. We are almost there." His words were long, firm, and drawn out. "Pay attention. You're almost there. We cannot afford to have anyone become negative at this point. Think about the Flock Mind, and we will get through. There may be a squall, though."

Bill pulled into the lead, and Gomer noticed that he started to glow. While he watched Bill flying, he saw that one of the other flocks was positioned a little bit below and somewhat behind their flock. Then the second flock moved right into position within the giant "V" of Gomer's flock. The two flocks were now superimposed one on the other. Gomer was terribly excited. He wanted to see what would happen to Bill when he dropped. He was thinking Flock Mind and noticed that the storm was getting closer and closer. Bill dropped, and now Professor Goosenstein was in the lead. Another flock now closed in near the Professor.

Yes, it was a storm, and it was approaching. The clouds were black and the winds were growing unsettled. There was a strange odor in the air which told Gomer that something different was coming. The marsh reeds swayed to and fro, swept by the breezes that were now a little stronger than before. It hadn't yet begun to rain, but the sky was dark.

Professor Goosenstein dropped, and three more flocks joined in the "V." There were now five flocks in flight, and Monica was the lead bird. She was glowing brilliantly. She appeared to possess a certain sweetness, a quality that was evident whenever she was in flight. She was gentle yet powerful as she pulled the flock closer and closer to the storm. Gomer couldn't help but wonder what it would be like to fly through a storm, especially the last forty miles, over the open ocean.

He thought, "Grand Goose will probably be right in the peak." He could actually picture Grand Goose flying directly into the storm. He could feel and see the fury of the wind. In his mind's eye, he could see the other flocks joining in, with Grand Goose pulling. Grand Goose was now a position higher than his own on the greater wing as a sixth flock joined the formation.

Ernest was at the point position as they neared the storm. They watched as the wind slowly intensified, then almost hesitated, and then grew fiercer still. As the storm grew stronger, they grew stronger. As the storm intensified, they intensified.

Ernest steered the greater wing in order to pick up Monica. Gomer heard Grandpa chanting behind him, "Flock yes, flock yes." Grandpa was really concentrating. "He's such a wonderful example!" Gomer thought. "He religiously follows all the Flock Mind techniques. His concentration is so keen." At that moment, he too started to chant, knowing that he had to concentrate to be at peak. He looked at Ernest and saw that he was glowing and then that he faltered. Bette was now in the point position.

Bette picked up Ernest, and a seventh flock moved into formation. It was an awesome sight—seven flocks, one inside the other, flying as one. It seemed as though the entire sky was covered with birds. Five more flocks were moving closer, waiting to come in. They were adjusting their flight and getting ready to join the other birds. One by one, they were preparing themselves to form a flock of enormous power and energy. Gomer was sure that the power of the Great Wing would pull them through. He was certain that the intensification he was feeling as each flock joined would increase and guide them through the storm.

The vision of Minion as the lead bird flashed in his mind. He saw Minion becoming the Grand Goose. He was celebrating with joy. He was ecstatic for his friend. Then he noticed that Bette had faltered and was dropping back. With that, Walter started to glow. There were now eight, no, nine; two more flocks had joined. The nine flocks were now flying with tremendous power, but the feeling was so easy. He remembered some of Grandpa's lessons about the intensification of power when the flocks join together to fly the last forty or fifty miles of the great migration together. He also remembered something that Monica had said. "If you're flying in one of the inner flocks, it is a gentle, peaceful feeling and very serene. It is beautiful to be able to fly inside the other flocks. You don't have to change position. Only the greater wing of the lead flock will still rotate."

And they continued to rotate on the outer greater wing, for one of these birds would become the Grand Goose for this migration. Somewhere within that flock, the perfect manifestation of the pure essence of the Great Wing was pulling the flock to the winter home. Gomer was very excited now. He could feel his strength increasing. He could hear himself chant, "Flock yes, flock yes." He saw August, Minion, Gracious Goose, and Grand Goose ahead of him. As he looked at Grand Goose, he felt very proud to be part of this tremendous greater wing. Just then, Walter faltered and dropped. Gomer could see ten flocks flying together as he moved up. Grand Goose was in the lead.

The storm was approaching furiously. It was racing toward them as they raced toward it. He knew that the moment of destiny for the flock was coming. The storm would unquestionably slam against them, and they would pull through together. Somewhere on the other side of the storm was their winter home. In order to reach it, the flock would have to exert tremendous effort while being guided by Grand Goose, who would surrender his entire being to the Great Wing. Gomer felt a touch of fear. He was praying silently. "Grand Goose, please stay in the lead until the storm hits. Stay there, right there!" He realized that if Grand Goose dropped, the lead would be taken by Gracious Goose, whom he also trusted completely. He wondered if Gracious Goose would stay at the point position or drop to allow Minion to fall into place and become the Grand Goose. Somehow, he knew that it was all up to the Great Wing and that the bird at the point position would simply surrender his will to the Great Wing. Somehow he sensed it would be Grand Goose or Minion.

The storm drew closer. The eleventh flock joined the formation. The sky grew darker. The harsh winds grew fiercer. The end of the marshland was within sight. Great gusts of wind were blowing across it, bending the reeds with immense force. He felt the gale grow stronger. "This must be a real storm," he thought. He then heard Grandpa say, "Flock yes," and saw August in front of him mouthing the same words, "Flock yes." He could hear the entire flock chanting in unison. He now saw Grand Goose glowing. The sight was majestic!

Grand Goose dropped, and Gracious Goose was now in the lead position of the eleven flocks. Gomer knew deep down in his heart that Minion would be the Grand Goose of this migration. He could visualize Minion guiding them through the storm. He was so glad that he wouldn't be it. He started rejoicing. He was thankful that he felt totally protected and totally cared for. He knew that the Great Wing had worked out all the details of the migration, to the last flutter and beat of each goose's wing. He knew that somehow the infinite majestic intelligence of the

Great Wing had taken care of them all and would see them through. In his own insecure way, he was thankful that it wasn't he, Gomer Goose, who had been chosen to be in the peak position as the storm intensified again.

Gracious Goose then suddenly dropped, and Minion was in the lead. At this point, only eleven flocks were flying in unison, and the twelfth was racing furiously to catch up. The storm had almost hit. The sensation was unbelievable. The power and the energy had increased to a level he never thought possible. He felt a new clarity of mind as he tuned in to the Flock Mind thought. He saw Minion in the lead. The eleven flocks were pulling together as one. The twelfth flock was near, and the storm seemed to grow even stronger still. Minion remained in the lead. Gomer was attentive to his glow. While in awe of this beautiful sight, he could hear August chanting, "Flock yes, flock yes." He was so excited! Grandpa was chanting too, and the entire flock was moving as one. Just then, as the twelfth flock moved into place, Minion dropped.

Gomer was shocked. He almost couldn't believe his eyes. There was August leading the flock at the peak. August was glowing magnificently! As the storm hit with full fury, August was in the point position and all twelve flocks were flying together, one inside the other. Gomer was chanting, "Flock yes, flock yes!" In his mind, he could now see the wonder of it all. He was celebrating for his friend, and he was celebrating the poetic intelligence of the Great Wing. He was also thanking the Great Wing for giving him the courage and energy to pick up his older friend August. Now Gomer understood why he had to make the drop and descend all the way down just when the flight had started. He had to pick up August because he was going to be the Grand Goose. Gomer could feel himself crying with tears of joy as he saw August leading the flock as the storm gained still more force.

And then it happened, the thing that he feared most, the event that all geese fear. August was faltering and dropping. At the point position, he had let go of the Great Wing thought and had faltered. Gomer shuddered as every lesson he had ever been taught flashed through his mind. "In a great storm," Grand Goose had said, "the point bird must never falter and must never lose his connection with the Great Wing, because if he does, it could mean the destruction and death of the entire flock or flocks, if many are flying together. He must never, no matter what the circumstance, falter during a storm. He must always maintain the point position at all costs. The Great Wing, on its own, will take care of his flight. Even the slightest doubt in his mind will cause him to falter." One lesson after another flashed through his mind. He realized that the entire flock was somehow being disrupted as August continued to falter and drop behind.

He heard Grandpa chanting, "Flock yes, flock yes!" He heard his own mind saying, "Oh no! What is there for me to do? What do I do?" Somewhere in the depths of his being, he heard, "Great Wing!" and he pleaded, "Oh, please, please, give me the strength!" In his mind, he heard the echo, "Great Wing!" and again he thought, "Please, oh please, for the sake of the flock, give me the strength, Great Wing!" Once again, "Great Wing!" echoed in his consciousness.

He felt a fierce power flow through his wings, and again he heard the thought, "Great Wing!" As he thought, "Great Wing!" he felt his energy increase, and he also experienced the gathering of his strength along with a certain clarity of thought, while in his mind he once again heard, "Great Wing!" He felt his strength grow further still as he pulled with greater force, praying with every fiber of his being that he would maintain the thought, "Great Wing!"

He could hear his grandfather behind him chanting, "Flock yes, flock yes!" He could hear the entire flock chanting, "Flock yes!" The identical thought entered his mind, again and again, and his mind seemed to be getting quieter and stiller as "Great Wing!" entered his being again and again. He could still hear the flock chanting, "Flock yes!" In his mind, he could see and hear every bird chanting, "Flock yes!" In tune with this, he heard, "Great Wing! Great Wing!" It echoed over and over. He felt his body take on a tremendous strength, and he realized that he was seeing the entire flock in his mind.

"Great Wing!" It echoed again. "Great Wing!"

He could see each bird. He noticed that August was faltering and dropping below. The storm beat furiously, and as it did, he heard, "Great Wing! Great Wing!" He knew that he would somehow make it if he could maintain the Great Wing chant. He knew that he could do it! He saw the entire flock chanting, "Flock yes, flock yes!" He knew that he was at the point and that the Great Wing was manifesting through him. He could feel that enormous energy again as he took on the storm, flying as the point bird. "Great Wing! Great Wing! I will! Great Wing! I must! Great Wing! I am! Great Wing!"

When the reality settled in and the experience became more comfortable for him, Gomer started to look around in his mind's eye. The Great Wing chant gently floated through him as he viewed the entire flock from within. He felt at ease. His power now awesome, he understood the Great Wing at a new level. He could now grasp the meaning of powerlessness because of the heightened power being generated by the twelve flocks. The Great Wing's power was penetrating his entire being to move all twelve of the flocks.

The wind had now shifted slightly, but with the Great Wing's power, Gomer was able to maneuver the entire flock, instinctively and intuitively without even thinking about it. He only thought, "Great Wing!" which really wasn't a thought; it was more like listening to the Great Wing thought within him. He looked down and saw his friend August in desperation, faltering and fluttering. He realized that he hadn't picked him up. He noticed that August was somehow much farther behind than he needed to be and much too far behind to be picked up by simply allowing the greater wing to descend on him.

Meanwhile, as August fell, he could see that Gomer was glowing. Gomer was starting to take on a certain majestic beauty. August then panicked and thought, "I've done it! I've faltered in the middle of the storm! I've dropped from the point position! I have left the entire flock in jeopardy. Oh, please, Gomer, please get the Great Wing thought going! Get it going! Flock yes, flock yes! Let me at least hold that thought." August was pleading with himself. "Let me hold that thought!" He could see his friend's glow. He could see that his little friend Gomer was leading the entire flock. He was still pleading, "Let me maintain the thought, 'Flock yes, flock yes!'"

Gomer looked down and saw that August was faltering and in his mind, he proceeded to move him. With that, August shifted slightly. Gomer realized that August was somehow still maintaining the Flock Mind thought. At that moment, August was thinking, "Flock yes! Let me see my friend lead them through the storm. Flock yes! Even though I've lost them, even though I can't be with them, flock yes! Even though I've dropped, let me at least see him fly as the Grand Goose. Flock yes! Please, Great Wing, oh, please, let me see him as the Grand Goose! Let me at least watch him, as long as I possibly can. Let me see the glow!" August continued to falter and drop behind. He noticed that the entire flock was slowly starting to fly in a wide arc.

Gomer was rooting for August, saying to himself, "Hang on, August! You can see me glow! If you can see me glow, just hang on!" The thought just kept flowing through his mind. "Hang on and we'll make an arc. I can see that you're still part of the flock." Gomer was feeling a deep compassion, a love, an empathy for every bird of the twelve flocks. They were all in unity.

The storm was blowing with fury, and yet Gomer's mind was still. He possessed a certain calmness deep within that enabled him to move the entire flock. This ease seemed too simple for even his own mind to grasp. It just happened instinctively. He noticed that he was swinging into a great wide arc. He could see his friend August, and he felt empathy and compassion for him. He felt a need to pick him up, a warm, calm desire to help his friend. "I can maintain the peak position," Gomer thought with confidence. "I will swing the entire flock around. Great Wing! Great Wing!" The thought continued to repeat itself. Again he realized that the flock was moving in a wide arc. "Great Wing!"

August was still watching. In the distance he could see his friend glowing. He realized that the flock had finally turned. He was now afraid that he would never be able to catch the flock on his own, especially since the flock had turned. Fearing that he would never be able to make an arc with them, he decided that he would at least watch his friend's glow. He would watch his friend's moment of honor in flying at point through this great storm. August continued to chant, "Flock yes!"

The storm was still battering August as he dropped toward the sea. Meanwhile, Gomer continued to swing the flock in a wide arc. Foot by foot, August's altitude was falling. He could see the ocean's waves lapping furiously. He knew exactly what fear was as he saw the ocean raging beneath him. He decided not to focus on his own fear but to concentrate only on his friend Gomer. He could no longer see Gomer, because the flock had formed its wide arc and the wind seemed to have changed direction. The flock appeared to be flying away from him. August decided that, in his mind's eye, he would continue to keep vigil on Gomer flying at peak. He would continue to see the twelve flocks flying as one. He was determined that even though he was going down into the sea, he would hold the Flock Mind in celebration of his friend's hour of glory. He would celebrate with Gomer. He would think, "Flock yes, flock yes!" and no matter what the circumstance, he would continue to fly as long as he could. He wanted to remain part of the flock, though he knew in his heart that he had faltered at the worst possible time of the migration.

Gomer was watching closely. He saw August faltering further and dropping closer to the sea. "Great Wing!" Now, just like an old friend, the chant peacefully rose from the depths of his heart and filled his entire being. "Great Wing!" He could feel the whole flock flying. The winds of the storm had changed slightly as he swung the flock around. He was still determined to pick up his friend, if August would just hold out. "Great Wing!"

August thought, "I'll hold out as long as I can. Flock yes! I want to be part of this, even though I muffed it and dropped at absolutely the worst time. Flock yes! I will be part of it for as long as I can."

In his mind, August felt sickened. His body was weak and battered. He continued to falter and drop gradually toward the sea. He knew that the ocean would undoubtedly consume him and that death awaited him. And so he kept focusing on his friend. "Flock yes!" The chant went through his mind. "How proud I am of you, Gomer. How proud I am. Flock yes!" The chant sounded within him. "You started the migration majestically by bringing me back into the flock, and you finished the migration nobly by being the Grand Goose."

Gomer was feeling even more serene. The storm had reached its final peak. The winds raged all around him, and yet he was still at peace and quiet in the point position. He was experiencing the power of the Great Wing within him while watching his old friend. Gomer brought the flock closer and closer to August from behind. He realized that August couldn't look behind himself and could no longer see the flock. He noticed too that August was battered and weakened. Gomer had to impel the flock to fly at maximum speed in order to reach his friend in time to pick him up. He knew that somehow it was being done through him, not by him. The Great Wing had worked out all of the necessary details. He maintained the thought of the Great Wing as he watched his friend continue to falter. He shifted the flock over and then down slightly. As August's flight slowed pitifully, the flock rapidly approached him. In its fury, the storm was whipping him around. Gomer continued to guide the flock closer and closer. He heard "Great Wing" continuously sound in his mind as he thought the flock gently down a few feet, then a few feet more, lower and lower. He passed directly over August. "Great Wing" echoed serenely within him.

August looked up and saw the whole flock passing by. He realized that the ocean was directly beneath him and his friend right above him. He could still see Gomer's glow. "Flock yes!"

Gomer thought, "If you can see my glow, August, think, 'Flock yes, flock yes!' Just maintain the thought. It's that simple." And still "Great Wing!" kept chanting through him. The Great Wing was illuminating his body as the chant kept repeating itself throughout his being.

Gomer pulled the flock farther ahead and then gently dropped it down on his friend. At that moment, August moved into the point position of the twelfth flock. Gomer could feel each and every bird in the flock. When he realized that his friend was safe and secure after being picked up, he felt the flock's strength increase. The point of the twelfth flock is the gentlest and most secure position of the entire flock. For August to remain there would require virtually no strength on his part.

Gomer heard the Great Wing chant sounding continuously in his mind, and he thanked the Great Wing for having picked up his friend August. He then realized that the storm was no longer as intense as before. It was slowly starting to abate. He heard the Great Wing chant and continued to move the flock. In the distance, Gomer noticed the horizon. He saw that at last there was land ahead.

Gomer swung the entire flock in toward the shore for the landing. He thought that his task was now accomplished. He decided to falter and was picked up as the last bird in the greater wing. With that, Grandfather Goose settled the entire flock down at Chesapeake Bay. They had finally made it through the great storm, and the migration was over.

17

The Grand Council

The Grand Council is a special time in the migration, because all twelve flocks take part in it.

When a very special Grand Goose appears and leads all twelve flocks through a storm, it heralds a time when a message will be given to the flocks. The Great Wing uses this Grand Goose as a vehicle for transmitting information simultaneously to all of the flocks. This message will be fully accepted by the flocks and will be used as a guideline for the further growth of their communities.

It was a festive occasion, and there was an air of celebration at Chesapeake Bay. The young geese were playing and dancing all around. Even though some of them had flown on the lesser wings, they still took part in the celebration. Because Gomer had led the twelve flocks through such a tremendous storm, everyone was aware that something extraordinary had happened and was about to be recognized. It was a

127

glorious time, a time that they would all remember. Gomer knew that he would speak tonight as the Grand Goose. He also sensed that the Great Wing would speak through him.

Gomer realized that the flocks would be listening to him in a way that he had never experienced before. He knew that each goose would be hanging on his every word and that what he would say would have an impact on many generations to come. Since he had no prepared speech, he knew that when he was on the platform in front of all the geese who had come to honor him, he would speak from the depths of his being and say whatever needed to be said.

Even though he was secure with the fact that the Great Wing would speak through him, Gomer was still somewhat nervous and afraid of being unable to speak before the council. He tried to remind himself, however, that the Great Wing would provide the right words, that from deep within him would come the knowledge and wisdom which he would impart to the flocks. Still, he felt powerless to do it on his own. Once again he sensed the need to surrender himself to the Great Wing. He reassured himself with the knowledge that the Great Wing within him would provide all the necessary words and would enable him to touch the hearts of his fellow geese.

Grandfather Goose presided over the Grand Council, which was made up of the twelve Grand Geese of the flocks that had flown in the giant formation. All of these geese had been granted the title of Grand Goose in last year's migration and had been invited to sit on the board of the Grand Council this year.

The Grand Council board meeting began. Gomer Goose was asked to stand in front of the Grand Council as the geese, one by one, walked by, thanked him, and expressed their appreciation. They thanked him for allowing the Great Wing to manifest through him, for permitting himself to be an instrument of its will.

Gomer looked around happily as he saw Monica and Ernest dancing together in the special way that only those two could. They flapped their wings and spun their bodies, moving in perfect unison. And there was Bill, full of energy, flying over the festivities and honking loudly, for which he was famous. The Professor motioned for him to come back down to earth. The formal portion of the Grand Council meeting was about to begin, and Gomer's level of anxiety rose dramatically.

It was a very special sight to see the twelve Grand Geese move into a "V" formation with Grandfather Goose at the head. Gomer was ushered into the center of the "V," and all the other birds placed themselves in another "V" behind Gomer and off to the sides of the Grand Council. They left enough room so that Gomer felt completely alone in the center of the two giant "V" formations. Slowly, Grandfather rose to speak, and the entire flock grew silent. He waited until there was a long calm before proceeding.

"On behalf of the Grand Council, consisting of the leaders of the twelve flocks, I call this session to order. This certainly is an honor, and I thank you all for allowing me to preside over this council. Our first order of business is usually to confer the title of Grand Goose on the birds who were chosen by the Great Wing to pull each flock through the fierce storm." He turned to face Gomer. "Since all twelve flocks flew together, we have the very special honor and opportunity to bestow the title of Grand Goose on you. We will confer this title from all twelve flocks in unison. Ladies and gentlemen, let us now proceed."

With that, the Grand Goose from Gomer's flock came forward and said, "I take back the name Michael and proudly surrender my title of Grand Goose to you, sir." He respectfully dipped his beak, and all the birds in the flock beat their wings and started to honk. Michael walked proudly back to his place in line. One by one, the other eleven geese came forward, surrendered their well-earned titles, and took back their original names. Each one bowed as he resigned, and all the flocks honked and flapped their wings.

As the twelfth bird of the procession approached, all twelve flocks started to honk in unison. The noise grew in a crescendo and became deafening as the last bird bowed and proudly returned to his position in the Grand Council.

Grandfather Goose raised his wings and silenced

the flock. "It is our tradition," he said, "that each of the birds of the greater wing step forward and give personal thanks to the Grand Goose. Because of the unusual nature of this migration, we will not do that. We understand that you all want to give your personal thanks. During the formal ceremonies, however, we will hear from Gomer's flock only." With that, Michael, formerly the Grand Goose, stepped forward.

"You have learned well, my friend—well enough to teach me. I am proud and honored to have flown with you. You bring dignity to our flock, and because of your courage we have gathered here tonight." He stepped back.

The Professor came forward. "Ah, yes, Grand Goose," he said, clearing his throat and looking around the entire audience, "this truly is a memorable occasion. You were in the perfect place at the perfect time, doing all the right things that you needed to do. I am proud to have contributed to your knowledge, and I am awestruck by your ability to apply this knowledge to your flight. Wonders do never cease. You have impressed me with your ability to take the lessons and apply them in far greater measure than any of your teachers. I am proud and honored to have been able to fly with you." The Professor bowed solemnly and then comically flapped his wings as he retreated into the flock.

Bill approached. "Gomer—I mean, Grand Goose . . . aw, shucks, I get so nervous when I talk to you now. Before this happened, I was never nervous talking to you." He paused for a second, as if he didn't know what to say. Gomer looked at him with a smile, and Bill said, "I still just want to be your friend." Bill bowed to Gomer, and Gomer bowed back, acknowledging their equality, and Bill walked back to the flock.

Walter stepped forward. "Thank you, Grand Goose, for not finding the convenient excuses that most of us would have used. Thank you. By letting go of your excuses and living up to your potential, you saved us all from disaster. The geese of the other flocks and I will be deeply grateful for the rest of our lives." He bowed and walked back to the midst of his flock, and a feeling of gratitude was present in the air.

Monica and Ernest stepped forward together. Each raised one wing, as if they were one bird, Monica raising her right and Ernest his left, and they bowed together. "Life is a joy, flying is a joy, and flying with you is a joy. We will always be grateful." They finished bowing, turned toward each other, and walked back to the flock.

The powerful Minion stepped forward. "Your courage and energy have inspired me to fly higher, farther, and faster than I've ever flown before. Your courage allowed me to be here tonight. May I also point out that your strength has increased enormously. We can all see that, Grand Goose. We can see your metamorphosis, the change in your form. What

you have experienced has made your body more powerful than ever before. It has been an honor to make
the migration with you!" With that, Minion bowed
and proudly walked back to the flock.

Gracious Goose appeared, as lovely as ever. "Your
name, sir, has changed, but your heart remains as
sweet and loving as always. I offer my respect and
gratitude to you. I lay them at your feet and thank you
with a sincerity that knows no bounds. Your heart has
touched mine, and your sweetness has touched my
soul." She bowed and then slowly turned and walked
back to the flock.

Next came Bette, who stepped forward with
August. Tears were running from her eyes and down
her beak as she and August bowed slowly. Gomer
bowed with them. He acknowledged, in his mind,
that they were wingmates for life, and he was pleased
that they were here. Bette started to speak. "Today,
my essence is gratitude. My entire being is filled with
it." She paused, emotions welling up within, and
began to speak more slowly. "I thank you with all my
heart and soul. I thank you for what you did for the
two of us."

August spoke next. "Thank you, thank you, thank
you. There are no words that can express the feelings
I have. My gratitude to you, along with my love and
admiration, will never die. It is because of your willingness to serve our flock that I am alive. I, more
than anyone, am grateful. You could have easily taken
the flock to our winter home without picking me up

after my fall. Again, I, more than anyone, am grateful." With that, August started to honk and flap his wings as all the other birds joined in. A tremendous noise ensued. Gomer bowed and acknowledged the applause.

Grandfather Goose stepped forward and told Gomer, "As the Grand Goose, you may respond to what has been said."

And so Gomer began to speak. "All that I did was allow the Great Wing to manifest and work through me. Michael, I am proud to carry the title from you, as I am proud to carry the title from all the other Grand Geese that flew in this migration. I would like to respond to my entire flock. Each of you has expressed the gratitude and appreciation of all the flocks. All twelve of you are my entire flock. Let me first say that what I did could have been done by anyone. It only happened because I was willing to turn my flight over to a power greater than ourselves.

"August, even though you fell from the point position in the midst of the storm, I never judged you as having fallen. I simply saw that you had dropped and that it was my duty to pick you up. As a member of your flock, it is my responsibility to believe in you, even when you can't believe in yourself. It was the Great Wing's way of finishing the migration. The flight was not under our control. Any one of you would have done what I did, had you been in my position. I acknowledge and thank our Great Wing essence for guiding me through the migration." Gomer paused, and the flock started another round of applause.

"I wish to give my personal thanks to each of you who flew and risked your life to help bring us all to our winter home. Every one of you has my respect, gratitude, and love." As he spoke, Gomer was wishing that he knew what else to say. Silently, he turned to the Great Wing within him. Silently, he acknowledged his powerlessness, and at the depth of his being he heard the chant, "Great Wing!"

Some of the birds noticed that he was slowly starting to glow. They were thinking about the migration, and the Flock Mind was still with them. Gomer felt himself beginning to transform. He felt a surge of power and energy coming from the chant. He started to walk back and forth in front of the birds and motioned for the geese behind him to move around to the front. And then he started to speak.

"It did not happen by chance that the storm took place during the last hundred miles of the migration. Nothing of this importance could ever happen by chance. You are twelve varied flocks with twelve slightly different traditions. It is time that we unify ourselves. It is time that we unite in order to learn the lessons of flight in synergy. For centuries, we've been making the migration, assuming that the only time that geese can fly together in perfect harmony is during the migration. For centuries, we've needed the adversity of winter and the struggle of a storm in order to realize our potential. We've been teaching

our young that to be a Grand Goose means over-coming tremendous adversity. We allow the seasons to control our willingness to use hyperflight and autoflight. These techniques have been available to us for thousands of years, yet we wait until the winds of adversity face us before we take the necessary steps to reach these altered states of flying. For centuries, we've believed that density could only occur just before a migration. We've believed that density was a phenomenon which was stimulated by those blasts of cold winds ruffling our feathers as the fall turned to winter and that we could become one giant flock only when density was achieved. We have focused on the differences in our values and not our commonalities.

"Yes, there were twelve flocks, each one represent-ing a different value, but together the twelve of us form a powerful unit. Each flock was necessary, rep-resenting its own special but different value. Each flock was flying in the perfect place at the perfect time. What does this mean to the individual bird? What does this mean to the goose who is pondering his existence and his ability to fly? Well, when you see that you have your values in place and that each value is in its proper position, you will understand not only what they are but also what they mean for you. You will be ready to use the techniques that were given to you. You will be ready to overcome any adversity. You will generate a power unmatched by any storm you could ever face. The entire direction of the flock will be changed by guiding your thoughts.

The twelve values represented by the twelve flocks are these:

"The first flock represents the value of honesty. The admission of honesty about the source of your power is an admission of powerlessness. We became honest about our personal power in relation to the power of the Great Wing.

"The second flock represents hope, the hope that we would be able to fly in hyperflight, the hope that the Great Wing would bring our flock to its true winter grounds. Without hope, we could never take to the air. Without hope, the thought of flight would not even occur. This hope was based on a belief that the Great Wing would direct our flight.

"The third flock represents faith. Without faith, we could never have started our flight, much less have had the willingness to surrender the direction of our flight to the Great Wing. The Great Wing essence will guide your flight when you apply your faith.

"The fourth flock represents courage, which comes in many forms. There is the courage to look at your present values and take inventory of them. The courage to stay where you are when in formation and assess your strengths and weaknesses. The courage to see who and what you are.

"The fifth flock represents trust. I had to trust Grandfather Goose and admit to him my short-comings in order to fly with the flock. Grandfather knew more about the lessons I needed for my growth than I did. He knew what it would take and what sort of lessons I had to learn, and he patiently guided me.

"In order for me to follow these lessons, I needed the sixth flock, which represents willingness. I needed the willingness to allow my faults to be changed and the willingness to take the Flock Mind training.

"I also needed the seventh flock, which represents the value of humility. I humbly beseech each of you, at this present time, to recognize that the Great Wing nature is alive within you and is always ready to remove your shortcomings. You can all see that I am glowing, again because the Flock Mind has never left you. It was just an illusion all these years that the Flock Mind would leave at the end of the migration. I humbly ask you to join with me in asking that the Great Wing remove this limitation from our consciousness so that we can enjoy the benefits of autoflight and hyperflight without needing the adversity of a migration to stimulate us. It is only your thoughts that are blocking density from occurring. Only the illusion that density has not been achieved is keeping it from you. You must persevere in maintaining the Flock Mind.

"The eighth flock represents the value of perseverance. I beseech you all to persevere in your attempts to understand the essence of the Great Wing within you, to understand your connection to the oneness and wholeness of nature, and to understand and let go of the excuses that limit you from seeing this nature in yourself and in every other bird of our flock. You see, every bird has the Great Wing nature within. Every time you offend or harm or hold ill thoughts toward another bird, you are holding ill will toward the Great Wing. I beseech you all to make prompt restitution to those that you have harmed.

"The ninth flock represents restitution. You cannot lose or gain any advantage over the Great Wing. You cannot lose or gain any advantage over another bird by giving or taking from him. Once you understand this, restitution no longer becomes a humiliating task. It becomes an honor, a labor of love. It becomes an offering to the Great Wing within another. Most of all, what you can offer to the Great Wing nature within another is forgiveness, our tenth value.

"When you offer forgiveness to another bird, regardless of the nature of the wrong they have committed or how they have harmed you, you are offering the gift of love to the Great Wing. This act will be abundantly returned to you. It will be returned to you in such an overwhelming manner that you will wonder why and how you could have ever held back loving forgiveness from your fellow geese. The power of love that the Great Wing possesses is enormous. It is beyond your belief. It is beyond your ability to conceive it. It is yours, waiting for you to forgive. It is waiting for you, at the depth of your being, to forgive yourself for the things that you've done wrong and to acknowledge that the Great Wing essence is within you.

"The eleventh flock represents your spirituality.

Maintain your Flock Mind. Maintain it for all the days of your life. Go forth with an attitude of oneness and harmony for your fellow birds, and once you've done that, the essence of your own spirituality, the Great Wing nature within you, will intensify. It will bring you a sense of joy and a great sense of peace. It will bring you an understanding that you are indeed truly one with your creator. You will realize that light, joy, and peace abide within you, that you are as the Great Wing created. This peace comes from that higher nature within you. Each of you has a part to play in the destiny of the flock.

"Your greatest function is to bring peace through forgiveness. Your part is essential in the Great Wing's plan to bring about this peace. When you are in harmony with the Great Wing essence within you and when you are in harmony with its will, you will find happiness. You share in the Great Wing's will. The Great Wing's will for you is happiness. The Great Wing is love, and love is happiness. You share in the nature of all happiness and all love. It belongs to you. Its peace and joy are yours. Know that you can rest in the Great Wing, and in knowing this, understand that you are of service to your fellow geese. Bring this message to them, and practice these virtues in everything you do.

"The twelfth flock represents the value of service. This service is the willingness to be a part of the Great Wing's will, the willingness to see that your will and the Great Wing's will are one and that you can be of service to your fellow geese through the practice of these principles.

"Many, if not all of you, can see that I am glowing! I would like for all of you to join in with me at this part of the lesson. The knowledge that I am about to give you tonight is being offered so that you can streamline the process of attaining hyperflight and autoflight. The ability to alter the mode of flying has always been within you. This process is very simple.

"First, you must admit your powerlessness to change the patterns of your flight without the help of the Great Wing. Second, you must believe that the Great Wing will respond to you in a very personal way. Third, you must understand that your own self-defeating thinking—the limitations that you place on your flight—is causing your fears and your anxieties. It is causing you to feel unhappy in your flying. Your thinking and the excuses that you make to maintain this thinking need to be released.

"Fourth, you must be ready to have the belief system that is maintaining your limitations altered. When you join in small groups over the next few days to enjoy the experience of hyperflight using these principles, you must alter your belief system so completely that its change will pave the way for the transformation of your flight forever. You must take that next step. You must decide to turn the care of your flight over to the Great Wing. You must surrender both your will and your false beliefs and request that you be changed at depth.

"The fifth and last factor that you must consider is forgiveness. Forgive and release anyone who has ever harmed you in any way, and forgive yourself for the mistakes you've made and for the limitations that you've accepted. Forgive yourself completely and allow the Great Wing to express itself within you.

"When these five factors are realized fully, you will understand intuitively that you are functioning in complete harmony with the members of your flock. You do not need a migration and you do not need a great storm in order to achieve this power. You do not need a great storm in order to be a Grand Goose, for that power is always yours. You need only to choose to be in perfect harmony and allow the Great Wing nature to manifest. Your flight will be transformed when you do this. The distances you will fly and the speeds you will achieve will change dramatically.

"The next two phases function almost simultaneously. They are the processes of seeing and feeling. As you start flying, you must see clearly, in your mind, where it is that you want to go. Allow the Great Wing to decide how you will get there. Do not be concerned about the appearances and outward circumstances of your flight. See clearly where you want to go and then assume the same feelings you would have if you were already there and had flown there at record speed. This point cannot be stressed enough. In your mind's eye, you must see the movement you want to create. You must see the flight pattern that you wish to be part of. You must have the vision of where it is you want to go, and then you must maintain the feeling you would have if you had already gotten there. The Great Wing will then take over and bring you to wherever it is that you want to go.

"Let us all join in and make a covenant. Let us agree that the Great Wing is giving us whatever we need in order to take our flight to the level of our imagination. Let us also agree that the Great Wing will give us whatever we want and need in order to complete our flight. Let us believe that the Great Wing will give to us what is necessary that as yet we are unable to envision for ourselves. Let us agree, in a state of perfect harmony, that the Great Wing is giving us the ability to fly. It is giving us all the skills necessary, even before we know that we need them. I ask you to join with me and dedicate yourself to live in a manner that will set the highest possible example for other geese to follow and to be an open channel for the expression of the will of the Great Wing.

"Go forth all the days of your life with the spirit of enthusiasm.

"Go forth in your flight, positively expecting that whatever you conceive and feel, in your mind, you will achieve.

"Go forth with excitement!

"Go forth and be at peace!"

Beyond Words Publishing, Inc.

Our corporate mission:

Inspire to Integrity

Our declared values:

We give to all of life as life has given us.

We honor all relationships.

Trust and stewardship are integral to fulfilling dreams.

Collaboration is essential to create miracles.

Creativity and aesthetics nourish the soul.

Unlimited thinking is fundamental.

Living your passion is vital.

Joy and humor open our hearts to growth.

It is important to remind ourselves of love.

Printed in the United States
By Bookmasters